HEYWOOD SUMNER'S WESSEX

HEYWOOD SUMNER'S WESSEX

selected and introduced by
Barry Cunliffe

Roy Gasson Associates

First published in Great Britain 1985 by Roy Gasson Associates
18 Ashdene Close, Wimborne, Dorset BH21 1TQ

ISBN 0 948495 01 4

s (Birmingham) Limited

l London

Frontispiece: Heywood Sumner at Cuckoo Hill, about 1930.
Copyright © Winchester City Museums

CONTENTS

PREFACE 7
HEYWOOD SUMNER 9

LANDSCAPE WITH PEOPLE

SUMNER THE NATURALIST AND COUNTRYMAN 17
Spring Pond on Rockbourne Down 19
Trees, and Anno Domini 24
The Common 31
The Forest 39
Note on Yew-Poisoning 49
Heath Fires 50
Cottage Chronicles 56
Pomona 58
A Winter Walk in the New Forest 61

IN QUEST OF EARTHWORKS

SUMNER THE TOPOGRAPHER 73
Earthworks of Cranborne Chase 75
Hambledon Hill 79
Castle Ditches (near Tisbury) 81
Badbury Rings 83
Buzbury Rings 85
Knowlton 87
The Mizmaze on Breamore Down 89
Earthworks of the New Forest 92
Buckland Rings 95
Castle Piece, Roe Wood 98
Sloden Hill-side Enclosure 100
Earthwork in Anses 104
Notable Barrows 107
The Old "Hedge of Ridley Coppice" 109
Salterns on Keyhaven Marshes near Lymington 112

THE SOLITARY DIGGER

SUMNER THE ARCHAEOLOGIST 117
Excavation of Barrows on Ibsley Common 119
The Romano–British Enclosure on Rockbourne Down 124
The Roman Villas along the Dean Brook 129
The Roman Pottery Site at Ashley Rails 136
Old Sloden Wood 141
A Potter's Hut near Islands Thorns 146

HEYWOOD SUMNER: His Archaeological and Topographical Bibliography 151
GENERAL BIBLIOGRAPHY 153
INDEX 154

COLOUR PLATES

Between pages 64 and 65
A bird's-eye view of Badbury Rings. *In private collection*
Excavations at Rockbourne Down. *In private collection*
A glade in the New Forest. *Collection of Mrs M. Hoggart*
New Forest view. *In private collection*
Farmstead at Newtown. *In private collection*
Sheep shearing. *In private collection*
Cuckoo Hill and the valley of the Avon. *In private collection*
Trees in the New Forest. *In private collection*
Danebury Hill from Broughton. *In private collection*

PREFACE

This anthology of Heywood Sumner's writings was a joy to produce and I shall be eternally grateful to the publisher for allowing me such an indulgence. I first became aware of Sumner's archaeology when, at the age of 16, I acquired a copy of *Excavations in New Forest Roman Pottery Sites* and, suitably inspired, set about trying to discover the kilns and the Forest landscape for myself. Nearly 30 years on, at a casual meeting in Dorchester Museum, the idea of this book was born, giving me the excuse to read and reread Sumner's entire works and to delve into his untroubled, but nonetheless gently creative, life. By a strange chance the reading and selections were done in the evenings during our July excavation at Hengistbury Head, on the edge of the Forest, and on trains between Christchurch and Oxford. Looking out of the train window I often found myself deep in the Forest landscape that Sumner so loved.

Here offered is a brief selection of what I consider to be the best and most typical of Sumner's writings. Much that is delightful and evocative has had to be omitted to present what is, I hope, a fair coverage of all aspects of our subject's output. For the most part the selections are continuous as published but I have, from time to time, removed long quotations, extensive references, or detailed descriptive passages. For the entire meal the reader is referred to the original books—think of our menu as *nouvelle cuisine*.

The completion of this volume has run in parallel with the preparation of an exhibition of Sumner's works, masterminded by Liz Lewis, Director of Winchester City Museum, and much of the more detailed research has been done while we were collecting material for the exhibition. The stimulus and good company of the exhibition team I gratefully acknowledge. Together we are determined that our hitherto unsung hero will get the recognition he deserves and that his works, both artistic and literary, will thus be enjoyed by a wider public.

BARRY CUNLIFFE
Oxford
3.xii.84

HEYWOOD SUMNER

Heywood Sumner, born in the gentle stability of mid-Victorian England, died in seclusion in the frightening uncertainty of the winter of 1940. His life spanned one of the greatest periods of change this country has known and he, likewise, responded by exploring, and indulging, his many talents, altering the direction of his life with surprising ease. Born into a family of churchmen, he trained as a lawyer, became a highly successful artist, and then, in early middle age, gave it all up and retired to the country to devote himself to archaeology.

George Heywood Maunoir Sumner was born in 1853 in Hampshire, at Old Alresford, where his father, the Reverend George Henry Sumner was rector. His family was deeply entrenched in the established Church. His father was soon to become Bishop of Guildford; his grandfather, Charles Richard Sumner, had been Bishop of Winchester; and his great-uncle, John Bird Sumner, was an archbishop of Canterbury. Heywood's mother, Mary Elizabeth, was also prominent in the Church—well-known as the founder of the Mothers Union. But in spite of this ecclesiastical background, after Eton, Heywood went to Christ Church, Oxford, to study law. In 1881 he qualified as a barrister at Lincoln's Inn.

But law was not to be his profession. At Oxford he shared accommodation with W. A. S. Benson, who was soon to make a name for himself as a skilled practitioner of Arts and Crafts metalwork, and it was probably through this friendship that Sumner was introduced to the world of William Morris and the Arts and Crafts movement. In 1883 he married Benson's sister Agnes and settled down in London to the life of a successful artist.

We know little of the transformation from lawyer to artist but an early sketch book, of English and Swiss scenes and members of the Benson family, shows something of Sumner's developing skills. More remarkable is the fact that in 1881 (the year in which he qualified at Lincoln's Inn) he published his first book *The Itchen Valley from Tichbourne to Southampton*, illustrated with 22 of his own etchings. This was followed in the next year by *The Avon from Naseby to Tewkesbury*, with 21 etchings. In 1883 Sumner was commissioned to illustrate Southeran's 'Artists Edition' of J. R. Wise's *The New Forest*, for which he provided 12 etchings. Throughout this time he was exhibiting etchings at the Royal Academy—his first exhibit (1881) being of the Iron Age hillfort on St. Catherine's Hill near Winchester.

Book illustration continued to occupy him. In 1884 he provided engravings for

Buxton's *Epping Forest*, but he was already involved in developing a more stylized graphic technique transitional between that of the Pre-Raphaelites and Art Nouveau. This he employed to good effect in illustrating children's books such as *Undine* (1880), *Cinderella* (1882), *Sintram and his Companions* (1883), and, later, *Jacob and the Raven* (1896).

Inevitably he was drawn close to William Morris and his circle and in 1882 he and Benson threw themselves with enthusiasm into the Century Guild founded by Arthur Mackmurdo. He was, however, soon to tire of the elitism which began to pervade the Century Guild and the Art Workers Guild (of which he was a master), and in 1886 he, together with Benson, Walter Crane, and other artists, broke away—intent on disseminating their art to a wider public. In 1888 they organized the first Arts and Crafts exhibition at Crane Street. Another venture was the setting up of the Fitzroy Picture Society, which involved a group of artists dedicated to producing boldly coloured pictures, usually of uplifting themes, that could be printed and sold cheaply to enliven the walls of institutions such as schools and hospitals, incidentally improving the minds of the inmates.

The period from 1880 to 1908 was Sumner's most productive time as an artist. In addition to his book illustration he rapidly established a reputation for himself as a sgraffito artist, decorating no fewer than 10 church interiors in the period 1884–97. A little later, in 1900, he turned his hand to designing stained-glass windows for the church of St. Mary at Longworth in Berkshire. Like so many artists of his circle he was not content to work in a single medium. In 1893 he produced the first of a series of highly successful wallpaper designs: more were to follow, particularly in the period 1900–5. All were based on floral motifs, the originals of which can be found, sketched from nature, in his notebooks. In addition there were posters (one for a Globe Theatre production), a linen banner for Malvern Priory, pokerwork-decorated furniture, and the design of a tapestry called 'The Chase', woven by Morris and company in 1908. As if to complete the picture of the all-rounder artist, he illustrated and published his own collection of English folk songs—*The Besom-Maker and other Country-Folk Songs*—in 1888.

Sumner was a child of his day—a typical product of the Arts and Crafts movement—ready to turn his hand to anything in the belief that the artist-craftsman should be a master of all media.

How then should we judge this prolific and versatile man? Certainly not as a great artist—his work, and indeed his temperament, lacked the drive and the arrogance so necessary to cross the threshold from competence to genius. Yet he and his contemporaries—Walter Crane, Aubrey Beardsley, Herbert Horne, Charles Ricketts, and Arthur Mackmurdo—were responsible for leading the British arts movement from late Pre-Raphaelitism to Art Nouveau. Sumner's position in the movement can be judged from the fact that his wallpapers were selected to decorate Horta's *Tassel House* in Brussels in 1892–3—the first international expression of mature Art Nouveau style.

How emotionally involved Sumner was with his art it is impossible to judge, since he did not commit his thoughts to writing, but suddenly in 1897, at the age of 44, he turned his back on fashionable London society and retired to Bournemouth, ostensibly because of his wife's ill-health, and in 1904 we find him buried in the wilds of the New Forest in his newly built house at Cuckoo Hill. A single wallpaper design (1905) and his tapestry masterpiece, 'The Chase' (1908), were the last commercial works he produced. He was later to claim that he had tired of the thrusting competitive world of London, but could it be that he saw his artistic ideals crumbling? Art Nouveau was to die a rapid death in the first decade of the twentieth century. In 1903 Lewis Day wrote that 'It shows symptoms not of too exuberant life, but of pronounced disease' and in the London Exhibition of 1908 Art Nouveau was hardly to be seen: throughout Europe the movement, and the market, had collapsed. It was a time of change and Sumner, now in middle age, seems to have lacked the spirit to cope. His loss to the world of art was however an immeasurable gain to archaeology.

The move from London to Bournemouth in 1897 was a tentative exploration of the south coast, though Sumner admitted that he disliked garden cities and had no great love of the sea. The family was a large one: Michael aged 12, Dorothea 11, Beatrix 9, Benedict 4, and Christopher 1. Together they moved into 'Skerryvore', a house in Westbourne that had at one time been the home of Robert Louis Stevenson, and for a while it served as a comfortable base from which Sumner could finish his remaining commissions while searching for somewhere more congenial to settle.

At last, in 1902, he found the ideal spot—Cuckoo Hill near Gorley, on the east side of the Avon valley within the boundaries of the New Forest. It was an area he had visited 20 years before when preparing etchings for Southeran's edition of the *New Forest* and it was to be his home for almost forty years. When he first saw it, Cuckoo Hill was simply a plot of land—'a squatter's holding on the gravel hills of the Forest, where we could try the experiment . . . of life amid wild air'. Having acquired it he set about building his ideal family house: the foundations of the first part of the building were laid in May 1902 and by April of the next year the house was habitable. Finally in January 1904 the vans of furniture from 'Skerryvore' arrived.

> Their arrival was memorable. They were delayed on the road, and did not reach Gorley till four o'clock. Then they stuck in the clay of the 'leäne' hill—immovably.

> There was nothing to be done but to unload them there. So Peggy, our old white pony, was put in the cart, and all the workmen on the job, and every one in Gorley came to help; then, by the light of a frosty moon, and of stable lanthorns, our household goods were conveyed in long and repeated processions to the unfinished house.
>
> THE BOOK OF GORLEY, 7

The arrival of the family at Cuckoo Hill marked a change of life for Sumner and he now began the second stage of his career as a countryman and archaeologist. But the transition was not complete until 1910, the year in which he published his delightful volume, *The Book of Gorley*, a scrap-book of personal reminiscences, country lore, local history, and shrewd topographical observation. It was a turning point—an apprentice's trial piece—which showed that he was now the master of a new range of skills and ready to make his special contribution in the world of archaeology.

His activities as a countryman, a field archaeologist, and an excavator will be considered below and will not concern us here except to say that between 1910 and 1930 he worked incessantly at his archaeology—no mean feat for a man between the ages of 57 and 77. Even during the First World War he found time to pursue his antiquarian interests:

> I am now an efficient private in the F. bridge Tr: Corps & we hope to be able to liberate better men as Time grinds on. Under no illusions of our military value. But we help to train the boys who will be enlisting when of age.
>
> It is rather humiliating to realize that I am an old buffer. . . .
>
> Pursuits abide and I continue hunting up N. Forest E. works. Last month, by rare good luck I got a fine Bronze Age Beaker from gravel diggers at F. bridge . . . .
>
> LETTER TO J. P. WILLIAMS-FREEMAN, 21 SEPTEMBER 1915

At the end of the war Sumner became an active member of the Bournemouth Natural Science Society. Elected an honorary member in 1918, he was awarded the Society's Morris Gold Medal for services to science and archaeology in 1924 and from 1926–8 served as its president. But, although he joined the Hampshire Field Club and Archaeological Society, and was elected a Fellow of the Society of Antiquaries of London, he took remarkably little interest in the development of archaeology at a national, or even a regional, level, being content to work, usually alone, in his beloved New Forest. For an elderly man whose main means of transport was the bicycle his output was formidable and his contribution to the discipline, as we shall see, was significant.

The publication in 1931 of his *Local Papers*, a collection of his general writings, marked the end of his creative life. It was a deliberate tidying up of the affairs of an active man who, at the age of 78, realized that the time had come to retire. In the preface to *Local Papers* he wrote:

> There is a town-man's quip that describes a countryman as 'buried' in the country. I demur to such grave location, and would substitute 'planted' instead, for planting is followed by growth, and the countryman who has health, opportunity, and understanding to pursue such local regard and research will be rewarded: he may grow old, but he will also grow up in mental outlook.

Sumner lived on in seclusion for another decade—still keeping up an active correspondence with his old friends, still faithfully recording annual rainfall figures, and still keenly aware that local history is a continuum up to the present. His last letter to Williams-Freeman, undated but evidently late 1940, is full of details of the intensifying war:

> We have so far been lucky, no bomb has fallen nearer than ¼ mile distant—(we feel bumps all round). One big and 8 small dropped within 200 yds radius. Damage—one well filled up—few windows broken, no human or live stock hurt—another lot of 7 or 8 fell in a field nr. Moyles Court with one hen killed. We have 2 dear evacuates, for the last 6 months. One 4 years other 7 yrs., girls and they have been joined, since Sth.ton has been so badly bombed by their parents and baby of 2 years. . . .

The active mind of the local historian fascinated by the detail of the history being created around him is still evident. A few months later, in December 1940, at the age of 87, he died. His breadth of achievement had been remarkable. He had mastered most of the artistic media of his day—painting, line drawing and etching, sgraffito, stained glass, and tapestry; he had then, briefly, become an architect and landscape gardener and had gone on to develop skills as a topographer, historian, excavator, and writer. At all he was competent and often original; at none was he brilliant. He was a man who matched well Aristotle's criterion of a gentleman—that he should play the flute, but not too well.

LANDSCAPE WITH PEOPLE

SUMNER THE NATURALIST AND COUNTRYMAN

One thread that runs throughout Sumner's life is a love of the countryside and an interest in its people. His etchings for the *Itchen* (1881), *Avon* (1882), *New Forest* (1883) and *Epping Forest* (1884) are the mature expression of a man for whom landscape, and particularly trees, are infinitely more fascinating than the works of man, and this theme of trees pervades his later writing as well as his illustrative work. In *Trees, and Anno Domini*, published in 1931, we are treated to what is virtually a hymn of praise, composed in old age. It is a reflection on change, the transience of life and continuity, explored against the backdrop of a forest. Yet woven throughout is a distinct, sometimes hidden, thread of pantheism:

> Both like and dislike suggest an emanation from trees that may arouse in us a dim sense of reverence, or of fear—of our being in the presence of unapprehended creations when we are surrounded by a crowd of old trees. . . . But whether liked—or disliked, they abide incommunicable.
>
> LOCAL PAPERS, 242

This same feeling, of hidden power reverberating from the land, pervades many of his writings. Of Spring Pond, for example:

> A great depth of transparent water inspires awe. . . . And now, here, this pit of Spring Pond is so unexpected, so abrupt, so deep, so clear and bubbling, that it seems to contain within it the wonder of a chasm—an opening as it were into the root of the matter, into the secret, hidden beginnings of the land springs—''Tis a ghastly place when 'tis full'—was the opinion of an old man in Rockbourne, and I agree.
>
> EXCAVATIONS ON ROCKBOURNE DOWN, HAMPSHIRE, 9

And again, of The Forest:

> So the years pass; and I, who also pass, say grace for this infinite creation dimly perceived but beloved, and dream of the secret revelation that will unite us to the sights and sounds and scents of Mother Earth.
>
> THE BOOK OF GORLEY, 91

Here, then, is the leitmotif that runs through Sumner's creative works.

Against this background it is a little easier to understand Sumner's somewhat unusual publication, *The Besom-Maker and other Country-Folk Songs*, a compilation of nine traditional songs collected by himself and published with his own illustrations in 1888. It was the first collection of English folk-songs to be issued since the appearance of John Broadwood's *Sussex Songs* in 1843 and as such is something of a landmark in this somewhat recherché field. It was an area he was never again to explore but nonetheless a reputable indulgence for a member of the Arts and Crafts movement who had a keen love of the countryside.

Sumner was a Hampshire man and remained such all his life. He was born at Old Alresford in the heart of the chalkland, but of the Hampshire chalk he wrote:

> I love it, but I do not love it as a home when the rains fall and the springs rise in the New Year. Then, during the months of January and February and March, the chalk white bosom of old Mother Earth is deadly cold; and the usual keen air, instead of being laden with infinite scents from miles of virgin downland, has a clammy breath, and chills to the very marrow.
>
> THE BOOK OF GORLEY, 73–4

For this reason when the family retired from London they made first for Bournemouth before finally settling on the gravel and sands of the New Forest fringe. For Sumner this was a totally sympathetic environment and it was from here that he was able to indulge his love of countryside to the full.

From the moment that the family settled into Cuckoo Hill in 1904 Sumner began to keep detailed notebooks, collectively entitled *The Book of Gorley*, of which there are three thick bound volumes. Each contains beautifully hand-written essays on a variety of subjects copiously illustrated with delicate water colours. Volume 1 is dated 1905 and runs to 1908, Volume 2 was started in 1908 but includes additions up to 1927, while Volume 3 begins with descriptions of his excavations on New Forest pottery kilns in 1917–18 but was still being added to as late as December 1938. The essays cover a wide variety of themes, from excavation reports and detailed studies of local history to local crafts and anecdotes, and even records of rainfall.

This compilation was a labour of love begun to celebrate the start of the family's new life at Cuckoo Hill and, appropriately, the first volume opens with an account of the building of the house. But what had begun as a private indulgence was soon to be made available to a wider audience with the publication, by the Chiswick Press, of an abridged version of Volume 1 in 1910 under the title of *The Book of Gorley*—the first, and in many ways the most evocative, of Sumner's antiquarian publications. The other two volumes were not to be published in full but most of the individual papers eventually appeared in print in journals, and the more significant were collected together and published as *Local Papers* in 1931.

The Book of Gorley shows Sumner at his most eclectic. There are descriptions of landscape—the Common, the Forest and the Chase—vignettes of his rural neighbours, country lore about heath fires and cider making, and several local history themes, all copiously illustrated with delicate pen sketches, almost naive in their simplicity but in a style now distinctively Sumner's own. So different is it from his early graphic work that it must mark a conscious break with the past.

The exuberance of this early writing reflects Sumner's excitement with his new environment—he was everywhere, observing and recording. But with the publication of *The Book of Gorley* in 1910 the phase of random collection passed and Sumner began to focus more and more of his attention on archaeological and topographical pursuits. Even so he never lost his love of the natural world and charming papers continued to appear from time to time. 'A Winter Walk in the New Forest', first published in 1925, is a brilliant evocation of the solitary man alone with his sharpened senses in a stark winter landscape. 'Trees, and Anno Domini', 'Latchmore Brook', and 'Three New Forest Hill-top Ponds', first published in *Local Papers* in 1931 but written some time before, all present Sumner, the countryman, at his gentle best.

For Sumner the first decade of this century was a time of settling in, essentially a period of readjustment between his life as a professional artist and his life as an amateur archaeologist. It was during this period that he learnt to study man's effect on landscape in the hills around his home and to develop a style of writing and illustration to communicate what he saw. The decision to publish *The Book of Gorley* may well have been a deliberate bringing to a close of this transient period.

SPRING POND ON ROCKBOURNE DOWN

Curiosity as to the remarkable water-source known as Spring Pond first led me to Rockbourne Down, and the discovery of the ancient site hereafter described was made in the course of planning the banks surrounding the Pond.

Spring Pond—as its name asserts—is a spring. A chalk spring. That is to say, it rises in winter when the chalk subsoil is full of water, and it falls as summer approaches, and as the water level in the chalk subsides; its sources of replenishment have nothing to do with the conflicting theories that have been advanced to account for the aerial supply of Dew, or Mist Ponds. It lies two miles distant from the village of Rockbourne; on the Western boundary of Hampshire; about 200 feet above the sea; and the subsoil of the surrounding land is chalk, capped with a shallow layer of mould. The place-name of Rockbourne is recorded as having been spelt Rochesburna (XI Cent.); Rechesburna, Rochesburna (XII Cent.); Rokeburn (XIII Cent.); Rogborne (XVII Cent.). The first syllable may be debatable, not so the second, and it is this with which we are concerned. A *Bourne* is the local name for a chalk stream that is intermittent in its rise. The word is derived from Anglo-Saxon—*Burne*—a brook. There are many such streams thus named throughout the South-Western chalk districts. For example—The Bourne, that joins the Avon below Salisbury. The Hurstbourne, a tributary of the Test. The Tichborne branch of the Itchen, that sometimes rises above Bramdean village. The Winterbourne that rises above Whatcombe, and flows into the Stour, and the Winterbourne that joins the Frome near Dorchester. All these intermittent streams occur owing to the nature of the chalk soil, which is like that of a sponge. It absorbs all the rainfall. There is no need of ditches to drain the land on such soil. Mother earth drinks in the rain until her chalk bosom is full to overflowing, and then at mid-winter she yields these crystal springs. Their flow is an index of the past rainfall, and varies accordingly, but usually the bourne that ran swiftly from Christmas to Easter, dwindles and fails before Midsummer, leaving only an arid bed of shingle to mark the stream bed.

At Rockbourne the main bourne spring rises near Toyd, and when it is running the village street is a very pretty sight. Little bridges lead across the stream to thatched houses, long whisps of water crow-foot waver in the water, while their intense green is shot by quivering reflections of many colours—cast by the cottage garden flowers. In times of summer drought, however, this village street loses half its beauty, for then the springs rise some three miles lower down the valley, the stream no longer flows through Rockbourne, and the little bridges look useless as they span a dry channel. But this latter is not the time of which I am telling, when the bourne descending from Toyd is joined by a field flood above the village. This has no regular watercourse and is evidently unwonted. If the course of this flood is followed up it will lead eventually to "humpy ground" in the upper valley, and here, surrounded by banks and sheltered by thickets is a great pit set in the spacious solitudes of the downs, brimming with transparent water that descends to a depth of amethystine blue; and this is Spring Pond.

Thorn bushes and grass tussocks grow on the sides of the pit, but these are now submerged, appearing bluer and bluer under water, as they grow nearer to the deep centre of this strange hollow in the downs. There is neither inflow nor outflow, but the bubbles ascending in little columns from the bottom, proclaim the living spring that issues five-and-twenty feet beneath the surface of the pool. It is very rare to see such deep clear water, and I do not know of any chalk spring, or water head that can compare with Spring Pond. I think of the springs at Alresford Pond, where amid the sedge on the northern side the water stirs and rises, and casts white sediment over the water plants—but these pools are only a few feet deep and across; or of the Hen-pit at Upton where at rare intervals rises one branch of the Test, to be joined at Hurstbourne Tarrant by another bourne flood from the Cock-pit below Walbury; or of Bridehead where the water of the

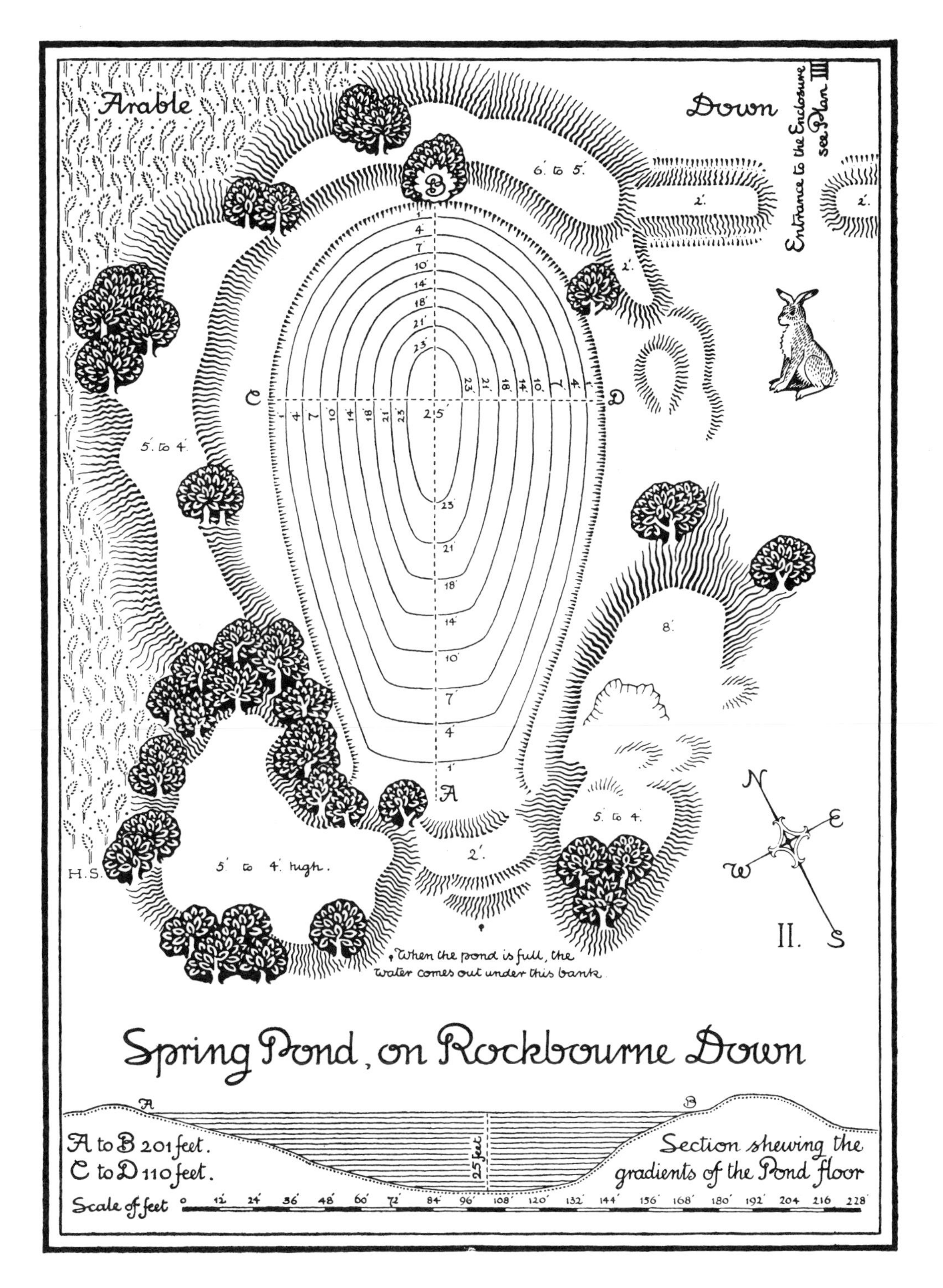
Arable
Down
Entrance to the Enclosure see Plan III
6. to 5.
2.
2.
2.
5. to 4.
8.
5. to 4.
5. to 4. high.
2.
H.S.
C
D
A
B
N
E
W
S
II.
When the pond is full, the water comes out under this bank.
Spring Pond, on Rockbourne Down
A to B 201 feet.
C to D 110 feet.
25 feet
Section shewing the gradients of the Pond floor
Scale of feet

Bride begins its course in a little lake, shaded by stately trees and circled by steep chalk downs—but here the water is not transparent to its lowest depth; or of Winterbourne worry, where the Winterbourne yearly up-springs in a little hollow among the trees near the "Ninestones." All these chalk-spring sources are memorable and beautiful, but they do not achieve the wonder of Spring Pond when it is full.

A great depth of transparent water inspires awe. After thirty years have passed I still recall visions of profound blue depths revealed in the Blauensee, near Kandersteg. And now, here, this pit of Spring Pond is so unexpected, so abrupt, so deep, so clear and bubbling, that it seems to contain within it the wonder of a chasm—an opening as it were into the root of the matter, into the secret, hidden beginnings of the land springs—" 'Tis a ghastly place when 'tis full"—was the opinion of an old man in Rockbourne, and I agree.

The wayfarer who has seen Spring Pond when it is full, will assuredly want to see it when it is empty. This is what he might have seen in May 1910. The water had then nearly sunk to the bottom of the pit. Thorn bushes that had been submerged in the early spring were now twenty feet above the present pond level, with green leaf showing on their whitened branches. The sides of the pond were trampled hard and bare by the sheep who had daily slaked their thirst in the sinking water—which was now reduced to slab dregs of the former transparent pool—while at the edge of the shrunken pond the chalk sides had been trodden into gray mud by the stabble of a thousand cloven feet. Presently a flock of sheep came slowly up the down valley; when the leaders were some hundred yards from the pond, they started running, and then the flock of five hundred ewes, each with a lamb or two at her side, poured down the steep banks, and this silent, solitary hollow in the downs was suddenly transformed into a live pit of sheep, baaing, and tinkling, and pushing, and wading, and drinking. For five minutes there was a ceaseless succession and movement of sheep beside the water, with a Babel of baa and bell sounds ascending. Finally when the laggards of the flock had drunk their fill, the watchful sheep-dogs came down, and waded far into the troubled water in order to get a clean drink, one of them swam across the pool, which showed that some depth of water still remained, and then both raced up the steep side of the pond, without waiting to shake their dripping coats, and resumed their constant watch over the wandering sheep.

A month later Spring Pond was quite dry, and remained thus till the midwinter rise of the chalk springs. Such is the usual rise and fall of the water in this pond.

For miles around Spring Pond do the sheep feed. Here distance is suggested as much as by sound as by sight—the sound of sheep bells gradually lessening until it is lost in the far-off downlands. Time is told by the labouring plough teams.

Spring Pond

From early morning they toil, to and fro, across the bare hills, then they cease—eleven o'clock, nuncheon time, and man and beast feed under the sheltering lew of bush or bank. Now they are at work again—It must be after twelve o'clock. So the brown furrows multiply, hour after hour. Now they are unhatching, and the teams file slowly homewards with eighteen miles of newly turned soil to their credit—It must be after three o'clock. Thus time passes here, and thus are the hours recorded, and thus do the great fields change their colours. In Spring, plovers wail, larks sing, stone curlews whistle, and March hares run their ringing courses. In Summer, harvest work brings an unwonted stir of life into the landscape. In Autumn, plough-teams toil, gunshots tell of the sportsmen, and the smoke of many fires tell of the clearing of the fields from coutch grass. In winter the Wilton Hounds will sometimes sweep across this open country. Otherwise, this is a land of solitude, exposed to all the elemental changes of the seasons, but set apart from the chances that transform so many parts of England.

EXCAVATIONS ON ROCKBOURNE DOWN, HAMPSHIRE, 7–11

TREES, AND ANNO DOMINI

It is a memorable experience to revisit the home where one was born and bred, more than seventy years ago; and to see the changes, in such respects, that the flight of time has brought about. Railway embankments of which one remembers the original construction, then, bare, chalk-white barriers across verdant water-meadows; now, hidden by self-sown trees and undergrowth, preserves for natural regeneration. Plantations, remembered as young saplings, now wood-lands. Fine clumps with landmark place-names, now reduced to stag-headed decay, or cut down. Hedge-lined roads along which one used to pass exposed to shine or shower, now sheltered and shadowed by hedgerow trees. Sights that evoke complex interest and emotion in such beholders; memorable; regretful; and yet pleasurable; for old age has its own special pleasures, as well as regrets, and the pleasure of seeing growth increases as years multiply, outweighing (to me) the regret of seeing loss.

Here, around Cuckoo Hill, South Gorley, where I have lived for nearly thirty years, there have been great changes during such period in respect of—tree growth—decay—and cutting—for example.

Towards the North and East from Cuckoo Hill lies the New Forest, and on this side of the Forest there have been many notable changes mostly due to Inclosure tree growth, *e.g.* at Pitt's Wood, the boundaries of which were reinclosed in 1903, and planted, principally with Scots pine, but such reinclosure and replanting mar the former wild beauty of this Forest bottom. There used to be a picturesque belt of hollies and thorns connecting Pitt's Wood with an outlying crowd of old oaks below Ticketsbury Hill, now alas, only existing in remembrance. But of this more anon.

There is also young tree growth that is interesting to watch on the hills and bottoms of Appleslade Inclosure—formerly covered with oak, sweet chestnut and Scots pine planted in 1828. It was mainly felled and replanted *circa* 1912 with Scots pine, Douglas fir and larch, thereby diminishing the pannage benefit of this Inclosure to the adjoining commoners. However, belts and groves have been left here and there, with groups of fine Scots and Austrian pine, that in years to come will be informing as dated tree growth, while the cutting of this Inclosure has revealed the varied rise and fall of the knaps and slades within its area.

It is interesting to obsèrve growth of this recent plantation, but forest lovers will look with keener enjoyment on the young self-sown seedlings, saplings, and trees, that may be found in the fine old wood of Redshoot, adjoining Appleslade. Forest timber renewal by natural regeneration is the counsel of perfection for handing on the present beauty of the old woods to future generations. Such process is most admirably shown (on this side of the Forest) by Anses—an old wood about 4 miles distant from Appleslade, up Dockens Water valley. There, beneath intermittent canopy of old oak and beech, protected by holly thickets and bramble brakes, young oak, beech, birch, thorn and crab-apple are springing up in every stage of growth, giving sure promise that the beauty of Anses will be renewed for centuries to come. Indeed, Anses is beautiful; both in the lie of the land sloping down in wooded glades to Dockens Water, and in the splendour and variety of woodland growth. Free-grown, upspringing, contorted, pollarded, spreading—every sort of imaginable tree-growth may be found here in reality. Moss-grown, ivy-grown, lichen-grown, in-grown, with honeysuckle crowning and festooning the lesser trees, Anses holds the secret of woodland magic—which, like most good things, comes by the way, by chance; here, the good chance given to seedling growth, protected by thickets in favourable soil.

But ill chance awaits seedlings in some of the old woods, where the woodland floor is feeding ground, or fern grown; nibbling stock and indiscriminate fern cutters are the principal enemies of natural regeneration. If the present state of things continues as heretofore in the decaying areas of Old Sloden Wood, Bushy Bratley, and Ridley, future generations will see dotards as the only relics of these old woods where such ill chance rules.

I wish that sweet chestnut was more planted in the Forest. It grows well in this soil, and when full grown bears and ripens abundant, mast, but its timber is held in scant estimation, probably because it reverses usual tree growth value which increases up to maturity. Not so sweet chestnut; its full-grown timber tends to become brittle and "shakey," but if cut at about fifty or sixty years' growth, its timber is almost all spine-wood, is very durable, and is unrivalled for posts and fencing (according to forest woodmen). Most of the sweet chestnut trees in the Forest are now far beyond their right time for cutting, and when they are cut will probably confirm the timber merchant in his refusal to quote a price for sweet chestnut timber.

Thorn, hazel, holly and (probably) white-beam used to be planted in Encoppicements and Inclosures, but such undergrowth is not of much account nowadays.

It is unfortunate that most present-day forest lovers take no interest in forestry for supply and profit; ignoring the fact (as shown by J. Norden's survey of 1609), that many of the old woods that we now seek and admire, are the results of past methods of forestry for profit. Those who protest against forestry for profit in the New Forest, and are convinced that the *only* objects of its administration should be the preservation of its beauty, ignore the fact that such change of management would contravene sections 5, 6, and 7, New Forest Act 1877; would affect a large class of forestry workers in this district, causing hardship and unemployment; and would destroy an historic industry of the forest, at a time when every acre of forestry is needed owing to our lack of home-grown timber.

During the War about 2,100 acres of Crown Inclosure woods were cut in the New Forest, and such vacant areas have been replanted with oak and beech, where the soil is suitable, and elsewhere with Scots pine, Douglas fir, larch, Corsican pine and Sitka spruce.

Scots pines are not inspiring growths to watch. They rise from bare woodland floors of pine-needles. Few creepers climb their resinous trunks. They have no remedy for mischance, nor for wood-wounds—if their foliage is scorched by a heath fire, they die—if they lose a branch, the loss is not repaired—if their leaders are broken off, they clumsily upturn the topmost horizontal branch as a substitute—and that is all they do to meet the changes and chances of arboreal life; whereas the resources and repairs of misfortune in all deciduous trees, and in holly and yew, are constant, and a delight to watch. They express tree-will to repair, to remedy loss, and to renew. Scots pine are bad losers.

Oaks wear the crown of old age in prolonged state, and when they slowly pass into the period of decay, such life as they retain is proclaimed in furrowed trunks, with few branches still bearing foliage, for years and years; until at long length of time, they gradually fulfil their tardy process of final transformation as hollow boles, with limbs having neither bark nor leaf, skeletons of spine-wood. There is much to be said in favour of occasionally leaving such dead trees in the old woods of the open forest, they supply unusual opportunity for regard, and record of the stages and periods of different species of tree decay, and they are preserves for natural scientists.

On the Northern side of the chancel of Harbridge church stands a grand old yew tree—12 paces within the churchyard Eastern wall. Its bole and double trunks are quite clean in bark, and free from shoot growth that sometimes covers the boles and trunks of old yews. This Harbridge yew has thrown out a great limb on its North-Western side, at 2 feet above the ground, which height has been thereby imposed for girth record of the tree—namely, 19 feet 1 inch. In structure it consists of two central trunks, surmounted by shattered ramification, and two great spreading limbs, with less loss of branching. The measurements in girth of these trunks, and limbs are as follows: The trunk nearer to the church, 11 feet 6 inches in girth, 6 feet from the ground. The trunk farther from the church, 10 feet 7 inches in girth, 5 feet from the ground. The limb nearer to the church, 8 feet 9 inches in girth, 4 feet from the ground. The limb farther from the church, 6 feet 11 inches in girth, 2 feet from the ground. The ramification of the two central trunks has been shattered by windfalls, and the remnant is scanty in foliage; but the two spreading limbs on either side, are surmounted by full foliage, such spread being from 11 to 10 paces from the trunk. Care is taken of this ancient tree—as testified by iron ties that bind its weighty limbs to upright trunk support. Long may it survive to tantalize successive generations who may question its age.

When first, in 1882, I saw Ibsley street fine elms stood on each side of the roadway, and the island, beside the weir was crowded with great trees, and enlivened by a busy rookery in springtime. Now, these roadside elms are either dotards or cut down; the island trees are getting fewer and fewer, owing to the yearly toll of windfalls exacted by South-Westerly gales on tree roots sapped by flood-water; and the rooks have shown their mistrust of the remnant by desertion. Indeed, the deserted rookeries are many near by. Throughout the length of Avon flow from North End—Harbridge—Ibsley—to Ellingham, 3½ miles, there used to be within the memory of old inhabitants rookeries at each of these places. Four rookeries, where now there are none!

The valley landmark of Ibsley has been a cluster of great elms beside the church, the street, and the Avon, and byegone Ibsley House. Decay, windfalls, and tree-cutting for road safety have destroyed this landmark, with resultant abiding loss. The scenery of this beautiful site in the Avon valley, is much less beautiful now than heretofore, and specially so since the fine wych elm avenue has been cut, that, for ¾ of a mile, shaded the high road from Ellingham Cross to Ibsley church. These trees were full grown, past prime, and the winter hurricanes of 1929, 1930, proved that they were now a real danger to the road traffic. A local keeper had his shoulder blade broken by a branch windfall in the avenue; four trees in this avenue were blown down in the 12th January 1930 gale, and two in Ibsley Park—one of which fell on William Grant's cottage, fortunately, without loss of life. These events quickened the downfall of the avenue trees (which had already been condemned by the county surveyor). The work was put in hand at once, and all the trees that endangered the high road here were felled by the end of February 1930.

Such loss to the valley scenery is, for a period, irreparable; but under present day ill-regulated conditions, unavoidable. So much traffic on high roads is now scheduled to time, *e.g.* motor-buses, and motor lorry deliveries; such traffic is obliged to use these roads even in the worst weather—to comply with time-table, when in the past all traffic would have been suspended until better weather prevailed; consequently the risk of tree-falls adjoining high roads is much greater now, than heretofore.

There have been many losses by windfall, and much decay in the New Forest old woods of Mark Ash, Old Sloden, Bushy Bratley, and Ridley during the last fifty years. Great beeches uprooted by storms. Outspreading limbs torn off from

H.S.
Mark Ash.

The road through Mark Ash.

shattered trunks. Old trees ending their days as moss-grown dotards, with strange fungus growths, white, brown, and spotted, growing above on dead branches, across crannies, and below in the crotches of sapless roots; while in recent years many young oaks have succumbed beneath recurring devastation caused by roller moth caterpillars.

Tree cutters are not miscreants, any more than are harvesters, or gardeners, or butchers, by whose summary acts we daily subsist; and letting trees stand—past prime—to old age and decay, is a luxury that few can indulge in; yet granting this, a felled tree is always a melancholy sight; a felled and rinded tree even more so, its naked trunk and limbs gleaming white against live green surroundings, like the bones of a giant woodland skeleton.

Rinding (that produces the skeleton appearance), can only be done during the few weeks in spring when oak sap is rising. A woodman (Ashton by name) who came to Amberwood cottage from the Forest of Dean, told me that they rind standing oaks there, and then fell them when the sap has gone back, thereby avoiding "star-shakes" in the timber; also, that rinding could be done quicker thus, *e.g.* he had rinded a standing oak in Amberwood in the same time as two men took to rind a tree felled there of similar size. Felled oak rinding has been the universal practise here, and I expect that our Wessex woodman would leave it at that, but "star-shakes" spoil so much timber, that such method of avoidance is worth recording—for verification, or contradiction.

The cutting of Cottage Plantation, South Gorley (spruce fir), in 1920 left no regret. Not so that of Newlands, near by, mostly cut in 1917. This was a fine-grown plantation of Scots pine, and its downfall is definite loss; but the resulting revelation of the steep hillside clothed with bracken and of the ridge bluff, terminated by a great barrow, are some compensation. Such loss is rarely as great as we may have anticipated. There is often attendant compensation in the results of cutting. "Wait and see" *is* sometimes a good maxim, in check of premature denunciation.

The clearance thus made in this (enclosed) wood, seemed to promise good opportunity for observing natural regeneration by self-sown seedlings. But now, after fourteen years' interval, there is hardly any. The woodland floor of Newlands is clothed with bracken—which is annually cut where the ground levels are favourable, but is left uncut where the hillsides are abrupt, and broken. The uncut fern dies down in withered layers of fronds and stems, through which, in spring, the young bracken crosiers push up their growth, and then unfold their feathery fronds, making fern canopy above the dead litter of past years below. No seedlings grow on such woodland floor—whether from dislike of dead fern litter or from lack of light when the live fern covers the ground. This being so I cannot suppose that fern cutting here has shorn off young seedlings that might have renewed Newlands. Outside this wood, towards the North, there was a grove of self-sown Scots pine, growing amid the heather of Ibsley Common. Heather is a good seed-bed for young seedlings, but is likewise dangerous growth in times of drought if heath fires occur, as was proved in 1927 when most of this grove was burnt.

Tree-cutting inevitably arouses musing in the mind of the old onlooker. It "amuses" him (in our forefathers' *musing* sense of the word) to consider his love of trees, and how they affect him. There is a curious sense of personality that seems to emanate from old trees. Antaeus-like, their being and strength is derived from Mother Earth. Rooted below, wind-blown and bird-haunted above, they fulfil their constant succeson of bud and leaf, of flower, fruit and seed, year after year, century after century; accepting elemental changes and chances, sunshine, rain, drought and storm, with persistent will to live, to grow, and to make the best of things. One cannot gaze on a fine old tree without reverence—the reverence due to achievement, to age, to a span of life so infinitely greater than that of any other living thing.

It is this dim sense of personality in achievement—of a presence inspiring reverence—that imparts pity and resentment at the spectacle of such a tree being felled. We behold the violent end of a woodland Being whose age may accord with a decade of centuries. This is the last act; when wedges have been driven to ease the final saw-cuts; and the to and fro rasping is resumed, and rasps on until the tree-top quivers, slants, begins slowly to heel over, and gradually—then abruptly the whole living landmark pitches downwards, with rending crack from the butt-hold, followed by thump of impact as branches, limbs, and trunk, crash together to the ground. We have been present at an execution and feel shamed to have been onlookers.

LOCAL PAPERS, 223–42

THE COMMON

There is a forest track leading from the Royal Oak at Fritham to Mockbeggar, and those who fare this way pass over a plain of scattered hollies on Hiscock's Hill; through ancient woods of oak, and yew, and whitebeam at Sloden; across miles of rugged heathland; past Hasley; past Ogden's purlieu; past Whitefield Clump; till the gravel hills abruptly dip, the heather stops, the Avon valley begins, and the Forest limit is reached.

So it seems.

But really the Forest boundary lies more than a mile back, across the traversed plain. There, on the edge of the gravel plateau, you may find bound-posts, if you search for them—the marking stakes of the old perambulations—few and far between—low gray posts, furred with lichen, and hidden with ling, but declaring with immemorial authority that here the Forest ends, and Ibsley Common begins—according to the custom of men, but not according to the habits of the beasts, the birds, and the green things that fulfil the days of forest creation; for they gain their scanty living where and how they can; alert, timid, and tenacious, yet without respect for the posts, and without fear of their customary bounds; for they—like the wayfarer—only recognize the limit imposed by cultivation.

The Crown and the Commoners, however, have agreed otherwise: so this wild expanse of unbroken Forest land has been divided by an unconnected line, which stretches from post to post, which separates Forest rights from Common rights, and which says, in defiance of Nature's contradiction, but with the authority of the Ordnance Survey maps—Here the Forest ends and Ibsley Common begins.

To a stranger, this separation between a waste of heathland called "Common," and a similar waste called "Forest," must seem to be merely the difference between Tweedle-dum and Tweedle-dee; but it is not so regarded by the

Ibsley Common

commoners, for the Ibsley Common rights are of more worth than Forest rights. For example: Common rights allow a freeholder or a leaseholder in the parish of Ibsley to turn out his cattle, ponies, or sheep without payment, to dig gravel, sand, or soil, and to cut turf, furze, fern, or heath for his own use in the parish, but I suppose with the reservation that the user must be "reasonable." On the other hand, a commoner has no right to shoot, nor to fish, nor to dig sandstone (of which there is a pit at the top of Brogenslade—"the Putts," or "the Pits," of the Perambulations), nor to cut a tree on the Common, but it is said that he may pull one up—a distinction which is supposed to prevent the Lord of the Manor from planting trees on the Common against the wishes of the commoners.

Forest rights are more restricted. They are of four different kinds:

Rights of pasturage: which allow the commoner to turn out ponies in the Forest at 1*s*. 6*d*. a head—or perhaps I should say a tail, as they are tail-marked as sign of payment—and cows at 2*s*., payable in both cases to the marksman.

Rights of mast: which allow the commoner to turn out pigs in the autumn at 2*d*. each.

Rights of turf: which allow the commoner to cut a specified number of turves without payment; and

Rights of sign wood—or assign wood—which give the commoner the right to so many cords of wood.

All which rights belong to holdings and to houses, and not necessarily situated within the present Forest area.

Every place has its antiquities, yet to write of the antiquities of the Common may suggest the inversion of ancient and modern; for the most ancient barrows and marks on the Common are new compared with its own primeval being.

Above Newtown, near Ladywell, and on Dorridge, the "humpy ground" records some honoured Celtic burials, but the great features of the Common were already old when these barrows were new; plains, whale-backed hills, and hollows like the troughs of ocean rollers, are the result of Eocene seas, of upheaval from sea-floor to dry land, and of down-rushing rains in the dim years of unaccountable period. All the change that chance and time have wrought on the Common has merely resulted in furrows that have deepened on its old face, and in hills more rounded beneath the elements. The marks of man, either in life or death, are scanty on this abiding wild that defies cultivation. The turf-cutter's spade still leaves its oval scar on the peaty grounds. North Hollow pit and Newtown pit yearly increase their sunken semicircles of yellow gravel. The cut fern tells of the thrifty commoner in autumn, and the gun-shot of the Lord of the Manor; while solitary figures all the year round seek for strayed cattle and ponies—as Saul sought for the lost asses of Kish—otherwise the plains, and hills,

Whitefield Clump

and bottoms retain their wild silence, and the habitual solitude of centuries continues. Possibly their solitude has increased. Certainly the trackways over the Common must have been more used in the British and Roman days, when the potters were plying their trade at Sloden; and the traffic to and from these potteries may have helped to make the deep "drokes" or sunken ways that lead up to, and down from the plain, on the north and south sides of Ibsley Common. I like to think of such an origin, though the waste of this soil under heavy rainfall is so great nowadays that I suspect my own suggestion.

On this side of the Common the water comes out at about the 200 feet line, and, if you look along our hills, you will notice a change of colour in the heather, running like a ruled line along their sides: above, the ling grows finely; below, the cross-leaved heath and sedgegrass dwindle in sour patches; and this change marks the line where the subsoils differ—where the gravel ends, and where the clay begins, and where water may surely be found. The highest springs on the Common are Ladywell, and the Source of Great Chibden Gutter on the upper side of Shab Hill. On the Linwood side (Ladywell excepted), the water comes out of the hills at a much lower level than on our side, and Linwood bog, beside the

Dockens Water, marks the outflow—Linwood bog, white with sheets of waving cotton grass in June, starred with bog asphodel turning from sulphur to deep gold, as it blooms, and then ripens its spike of seed-vessels, scented with sweet-gale, haunted by snipes and plovers, channelled with little peaty gutters that drip into the Dockens Water all through the long Midsummer days of drought. Here is the cause why the Dockens Water flows when the Hucklesbrook on the other side of the hill is as dry as the brook Cherith; for, when summer parches old Mother Earth, the overflow of our hill springs is sucked up by the thirsty land, long before it can reach the distant brook.

Both these streams that I have mentioned—the Dockens Water and the Hucklesbrook—flow in little shelving deeps, and in gravelly shallows, over which the clear water runs, amber and brown, the natural home for spawning salmon. So you would think, but although the great fish come up the Avon as far as Fordingbridge, they do not now turn aside on the way. Thirty years ago the salmon used to spawn up along these Forest streams, and a story is minded here how a great 20 lb. fish was caught one Sunday morning, just below the cattle stop near Blunt's Barn; but when the powder mills were first established at Eyeworth, the water of the Hucklesbrook was fouled, the cattle would not drink it, and the

The Dockens Water

Rockford Common

Newlands Bridge

fish floated dead in the stream. This nuisance was stopped long ago, but although the water has been uncontaminated for many years, the salmon have never returned, and even small fish are scarce. The Dockens Water is fairly supplied with small trout, and kingfishers haunt this stream, but they are not so often to be seen on the Hucklesbrook.

The wild animal life on the Common is much the same as that to be found in the Forest. Roaming fallow deer sometimes harbour at Leadenhall, and I have seen them near Newland's Bridge. Foxes have earths at Foxholes, above Brogenslade, on the south-eastern side, and at Shab Hill—where I have seen one—badgers occasionally come down from the Forest. Hares are few; rabbits are plentiful; stoats and weasels survive in spite of the keepers; partridges and pheasants out-lie from the preserves in the valley; curlews come up from the sea in May for nesting; snipes are frequently in Linwood bog, and occasional on our brook; wild duck sometimes nest in Great Chibden Bottom, and in May they walk their brood down the leäne to the Hucklesbrook, and so on to the Avon, with quacking fuss, and frabble if they are interrupted in their exodus; nightjars abound in May and June; glow-worms light up on Cuckoo Hill in July when the

Great Chibden Bottom

nightjars have almost ceased to churr; grass-snakes and slow worms are common; adders and lizards occasional; and we have also the smooth snake (*coronella austriaca*) which is peculiar to the New Forest and the heathlands south of the Avon. A very large one, a female, three foot long, was killed on our front drive. This smooth snake is harmless, but hisses and darts in a way that suggests venom.

THE BOOK OF GORLEY, 10–22

THE FOREST

The Forest suggests trees; green tracks through interminable trees; above, waving branches; below, tree trunks and tangle; broken visions of multitudinous tree tops on wooded hills, and shadowy gloom as the trees descend the valleys. Up hill and down dale trees, innumerable trees.

But this does not describe our side of the Forest. Here, on the northern side—and the Ringwood and Romsey road may be taken as the boundary between the north and south sides of the Forest—here we have long rolling hills, capped with plateau gravel and clothed with heather, fern, and furze, worn into five parallel ridges and furrows by streams that trickle in dry, and rush in wet

A Forest stream.

weather, down gravelly courses to the broad valley of the Avon. Here and there the hills are covered with thickets of holly, thorn, yew, and crab-apple; with old woods of oak, beech, yew, holly, thorn, and whitebeam; and with enclosures of Scots pine, larch, oak, and sweet chestnut. But the main features of our side of the New Forest are heather uplands, winding moorland streams, and scattered woods. The open country is never far distant. Afoot or awheel you may learn the same thing. The tracks from Highwood and Ogdens and Frogham leading to Fritham, and the roads from Ringwood and Fordingbridge and Downton leading to Cadenham, all give far views, over wild foregrounds, to distant cultivation. They reveal the vision of a primeval waste, set in the midst of an older and more fertile formation: of heathlands surrounded by the chalk hills of Dorset, Wilts, Hants, and the Isle of Wight: and from the lie of the land and from the vegetation, you may know that the Bagshot and Bracklesham Beds on which you stand are deposited over a great trough of chalk that dips from Badbury and Pentridge to "the Island," and from Purbeck to the Hampshire South Downs.

"Praise the sea, but keep on land," says the old proverb. "Praise the chalk, but keep on gravel," is a later version in my Book of Wisdom.

I was born and bred on Hampshire chalk, and I love it, but I do not love it as a home when the rains fall and the springs rise in the New Year. Then, during the months of January and February and March, the chalk white bosom of old Mother Earth is deadly cold; and the usual keen air, instead of being laden with infinite scents from miles of virgin downland, has a clammy breath, and chills to the very marrow.

Here, our coldest winds in the early year come from the great chalk uplands of Cranborne Chase, which bound our distant view in the west and north-west. But we escape the ground cold of that soil. The winds may be keen, but they do not search rheumatic bones; and for the rest of the year they bring us that fine quality of air that seems to be specially distilled from the chalk as the breezes pass over its ancient coat of turf, sheep-trimmed, and patterned with cowslips and thyme and milkwort and bird's-foot trefoil.

Thus we live on gravel, and praise the chalk; and our Benedicite is shared by all the Forest cattle; they know where the winds blow refreshment, for their summer shades are on the open plains, above the sluggish air of the shut-in valleys. On Godshill and Latchmoor, at Longcross and Ocknell, at Handycross and Broomy, the ponies and foals and tinkling cows stand through the hot hours of midsummer days, cooled by the breezes that come from the chalk-land; and so, by their choice, they also praise this airy gift of the distant hills.

The Forest ponies that live among these hills and valleys and old enclosures seem to be just as wild and indigenous as their surroundings. They are wild, in so

Forest Ponies

far as they are unbroken, and only to be caught by hunting them. But they are all owned. The agister would tell you by whom, and, further, he would tell you where every pony should "haunt." That is his business. He it is who collects the modest payment of eighteenpence, which is the yearly fee for a pony from those owners who have Forest rights. Only eighteenpence a year! And this for the keep of a mare who may make you a yearly present of a foal! Surely, you think, it must pay to keep Forest ponies. So it would seem; yet when first we came here I was surprised to find that none of our small farmers had ponies up in the Forest. They had tried it, they said, and it did not pay. The ponies came down, strayed on the highway, were pounded; in short, were more trouble than they were worth. I wondered. Now, however, I know that they are right. If Forest ponies are to pay, you must either be specially situated in the heart of the Forest, or you must have rough pastures handy when feed runs short in the winter, or you must pick them up at very low prices. For example: Forest mares that are good "haunters" (*i.e.* that do not stray from their usual feeding place) cost about £8 apiece. With luck

Sloden Hill

you get two foals in three years from each mare. These fetch from £2 to £3 10*s.*, sold at five months old as suckers. A mare has, say, nine years of breeding life, during which time she may have six foals, of which you keep one filly foal to take her place as a brood mare. That leaves five suckers sold at an average of say £2 10*s.*=£12 10*s.* From this deduct 13*s.* 6*d.* for nine years tail-marking. This leaves £11 16*s.* 6*d.* That is £3 16*s.* 6*d.* profit on £8 spread over nine years. But this computation is really much too liberal. It supposes that you pay nothing for driving in your colts, that everything goes right with your mare and her six foals, and that she costs you nothing extra for feed during a hard winter. Again, if your mare comes down from the Forest and strays, you soon spend both time and shillings in finding the wanderer, as, for instance, I spent a week and ten shillings in the spring of 1906 finding a mare whose thoughts had lightly turned to love, and thereby had been misled to Woodlands, nine miles from here. And thus your margin of profit may vanish. The "poundage" fine in the case of strayed ponies is 4*d.*, and the pound-keeper has no right to demand damages; that must be done by the person who has sustained the damage (Verderer's Court, Nov. 19, 1906). At the same court Mr. Evans said that he had spent £1 9*s.* 6*d.* in 1905 reclaiming one mare and colt!

The larger owners of Forest ponies generally turn out a stallion, and the mares are thus served free and by chance; but the chance has been much improved of late by the "Association for the Improvement of the Breed of New Forest Ponies," which holds an annual show in the spring at Lyndhurst, and which gives premiums and prizes for the best pony sires that are to run in the Forest, while the breed is further helped by "The Burley and District New Forest Pony and Cattle Society," the chief aim of which is to improve and to encourage the breed of Forest mares.

Here, we keep our mares partly out on the Common and partly in, using them for six months of the year; and the better feed and care which they get commands a better price for their foals. (I have sold three suckers for £6 10*s.*, £6, and £5 10*s.* respectively.) But this breeding is limited by the feed on the Common, and no one keeps more than two or three mares under these local conditions.

Besides the ponies, fallow deer are the principal wild occupants of the Forest. Ponies—Deer. Surely the order should be inverted. Surely the deer and the Forest are cause and effect. The Forest exists because of the deer, and the ponies are intruders. So you would think, but there is reason in the order which I have adopted. The deer have been dispossessed. Since the Deer Removal Act of 1851, they are supposed to have been exterminated. The remnant of the ancient herds only exist on sufferance, and the ponies now legally roam in their stead. Truly a democratic vista, and a topsy-turvy event to grow out of the stern Forest laws of William the Conqueror.

In the article on Fallow Deer, by Mr. Gerald Lascelles, in the *Victoria History of Hampshire* (written in 1900), he estimates their number in the Forest as about 200, more or less; but of late years they have increased considerably. There are four special haunts of the deer on our northern side of the Forest—Roe (including Pinnick, Redshoot, and Milkham), Slufters, Holly Hatch and Anses, Island's Thorn and Amberwood. If you know where to look for them you will rarely be disappointed. The year 1906 was an acorn year, and the deer congregated in the oak woods. More deer were in Roe during that autumn and winter than had been known for years. A herd of fifty-seven was seen, and the keeper put the number of fallow deer haunting in Roe, Pinnick, and Milkham at more than 100. I saw a herd of twenty in Pinnick, and a herd of eighteen in Holly Hatch; so the deer still thrive in spite of their extermination!

When their number gets up, as it has now, they are shot by the keepers with grape shot as well as hunted by the deerhounds, and when they trespass and damage crops the Forest farmers also shoot them. I remember staying at Goulding's at Highwood Farm in 1899, and after eating venison for supper, I asked where it came from. "Shot on my farm. Mr. Lascellas" (so he pronounced Lascelles) "he come and says: 'Goulding, I'm told you've a-been shooting deer, you mussen do it'. 'Who's a-going to stop me, if they come on my land?' 'Well,' he says, 'you mussen shoot the deer.' 'Who's a-going to stop me?' I says. 'Well,' he says, 'you mussen do it, and I shall tell on you to 'his 'Lardship.' So the next time I pays my rent, I sent his Lardship a haunch, and told 'en that I coulden keep the deer off my land, and he never said nothing." And this confirmed Goulding in his interrogatory creed, "Who's a-going to stop me?" Legally, I believe, the deer are supposed to have been exterminated, and so no one can stop you from shooting these outlawed survivals on your own grounds. Long may they survive to complete the wild beauty of their haunts.

As to the red deer, only a poor remnant remains to testify of the past. There were seven hinds, two stags, and a brocket known to be on this side of the Forest in 1906–1907, and I saw the stags and the brocket in Anses in the autumn of 1906. Since then I believe they have increased. I have never seen roe deer in the Forest, but there are said to be some occasionally strayed from Dorset, where they are fairly plentiful, especially on the wooded slopes and combes of Bulbarrow, where I have twice seen them.

The two harvests of the Forest are fern and holly—ferning in the autumn, hollying in the winter. The fern is cut by the Forest men and carried by the buyers. A load of fern delivered here costs 8*s*., and the loads are full measure, twelve feet high from the ground, bonded in the loading, corded, and then the moving brown stacks creak slowly homeward along the rutty Forest tracks, to supply litter for the small farmers who are not men of straw.

Forest litter is the coarse grass cut in the enclosure sides, and this also we buy of the Forest men. A load delivered here costs 9*s*.

Hollying begins at the end of November. The holly trees are chosen and cut in each walk by the woodmen. Then the man who has undertaken to buy the holly cuts up the felled trees into "Forest faggots" (twelve bundles go to a faggot), for which he pays £10 per 100 faggots to the Crown. John Thomas of Furze Hill takes Burley Walk, and he and his five helpers aim at cutting up, tying, and carting home to Gorley thirty faggots a day. And this continues for the fortnight during which the work lasts. All the holly is then taken to the nearest station and trained up to Nine Elms Yard, where it is sold to the various buyers. A forest faggot is said to cost the seller about 5*s*. by the time it is on sale in London, and the trade sale price varies from 5*s*. 6*d*. to 6*s*. 6*d*. This year (1907) some of the holly was poor stuff, with few berries, and hollyers lost money; £60 is said to have been lost by a

H.S.

man at Bartley. The Crown deals well with its holly tenants, and an old hollyer continues, year after year, to get the walk which he has been wont to take. John Thomas tells of a man "from up-along, who wanted terrible to get into the business, so he wrote to the Crown and bid £12 a hundred faggots, instead of the £10 which we do give. But the Crown told en that they must first satisfy their old customers, and then he mid have the holly that wasn't wanted at the price he named, so he got our leavings dear."

The cultivation and maintenance of the woods as timber tree enclosures, and their ultimate development into the hazard and freedom of the old woods are debatable subjects. The preservation of the wild beauty of this tract of land as we now see it is the constant but vain desire of a Forest lover—vain, because this wild beauty does not exist owing to the forethought and set intention of past generations, but it has grown by chance and custom, working within the bounds of shifting laws and of their varied enforcement. In dealing with wild nature, you need a large acceptance of temporary ruin, and you must think and see in centuries. The spoil banks and pottery refuse at Sloden must once have been ugly blotches on the hillside. Now their rise and fall add richness and variety to the contours of the heath land. Cerdic's great camp above the Avon at Castle Hill must once have arisen as raw earthworks of tipped clay and gravel and sand beside the swampy reaches of the Avon. Now it adds grandeur to the riverside, and witnesses, amid thickets of thorn and merry trees, to the fierce days of the sixth century, when the Britons, led by Ambrosius, fought the West Saxons at Cerdic's ford close by. Thus is our landscape fashioned. Time and chance are the makers of wild beauty. It comes by the way. Here the sagacity of Polonius will not avail, and the advice of the book-learned will be in vain, for the Forest lives and dies and revives again because of this, and in spite of that, with the law and outside the law, while eventually Nature always controls the hidden upshot.

Well, I have now given some account of our side of the Forest, though neither words nor pictures can convey the charm, the variety, the monotony, the tenacity of the life that abides in these wild places. The heather passes from dun to sombre green, then blooms in purple, and withers to rusty gray. The bracken push up croziers in May, make patchwork of green on the dark hillsides through the summer, of yellow through the autumn, of brown through the winter. The bog-myrtle flowers in dull red and rust, then comes into fragrant leaf, then gilds the gravelly streams with borders of gold. The furze passes from flowery radiance to prickly dulness. The bog-moss passes from green to yellow, to orange, to red; the mat-grass from glaucous to sandy green; and the woods—the woods pass from the infinite variety of winter branch and bud colour to the brightness of spring, to the fulness of summer, to the splendour of autumn. So the years pass;

Anses

Palmers Slough

and I, who also pass, say grace for this infinite creation dimly perceived but beloved, and dream of the secret revelation that will unite us to the sights and sounds and scents of Mother Earth.

THE BOOK OF GORLEY, 73–91

NOTE ON YEW-POISONING

The foliage of some of the small yew trees in Sloden is nibbled round so close as to give the effect of clipped bushes. I once asked Broad, the woodman, of Amberwood Cottage (now "superannivated") whether he had ever observed ill-effects from such yew browsing. Only once, he said, when during a frosty spell he found three deer dead beside some yew boughs that had been broken down by the snow. The foliage of the broken boughs and the slots of the deer showed that they had been feeding on the yew. From this Broad deduced (wrongly, as I believe) that the top boughs of yew were poisonous, and not the lower ones. The deer probably died from eating yew on an empty stomach.

"From the experiments of Professor Wiborg, it appears that yew-leaves, eaten alone, are fatal to animals, particularly to horses; but that when mixed with twice, or thrice as much oats, they may be used without danger. This neutralisation of the poisonous qualities of the yew by another vegetable may explain, to a certain extent, the diversity of opinion upon their effects; it being possible that some animals, which have eaten of the yew without inconvenience, had shortly before eaten heartily of some other vegetable."—Loudon, *Arboretum et Fruticetum*, vol. iv, pp. 2089–90.

The experience of Mr. Elias Pitts Squarey of The Moot, Downton, confirms this conclusion, and he told me the following stories as examples. Fonthill Park is full of yews, and the cattle that are wont to be turned out there nibble the yews and never suffer. In Basildon Park, near Reading, there are likewise many yew trees, and the owner used to take in cattle, driven from a distance, on their way to the Reading market. He had to discontinue so doing, as many of the cattle died from the ill-effects of yew browsing. They ate yew on an empty stomach.

Again, Louisa, Dowager Lady Ashburton of Melchet Court, had to send for her coal to Romsey, seven miles distant. A horse that had just returned with a cartload of coal was left, before unhatching, in a yard overhung with yews. He misspent his off time browing on the yew sprays, and in two hours the horse died. The yew was eaten on an empty stomach.

Mr. Squarey has often noticed his own well-fed cows nibbling the yew trees about his place, but has never known them to suffer from so doing.

Mr. Champion Russell, of Stubbers, Essex, tells me: "My only personal experience is, that a horse of mine died after feeding on lawn-mowings which chiefly consisted of dry fallen yew leaves. It is generally supposed that yew is much more poisonous when wilted, *i.e.*, dried."

Loudon also refers to this opinion that withered yew leaves are more poisonous than green.

THE BOOK OF GORLEY, 123–4

HEATH FIRES

During the first three years of our life at Cuckoo Hill there were no heath fires on Ibsley Common. Occasionally furze bushes were set alight on Gorley Hill, but they only made a grand blaze, and died down after creating mild excitement, leaving a small blackened patch as the morning record of what seemed to be a great fire on the preceding night.

Fires, also, we had seen every spring, far up in the Forest, or across the valley on the Plumley, Verwood, and St. Ives heathlands—some authorized burnings, such as the great furze fire on Latchmoor on Easter Monday, 1905, some unauthorized, by accident on purpose—but the fires had never come near us, nor did we know the dangerous speed of a heath fire running before the wind till the spring of 1906, when a tract of Ibsley Common was burnt from end to end—from Dorridge to Newlands—and this is how it came about.

Furze Hill was the starting point. Furze Hill is rightly named, and of late years the Commoners were complaining that the furze had made too much growth; it was encroaching on the feed. Accordingly, a petition was addressed to Lord Normanton, the Lord of the Manor, thus:

March 12, 1906.

To E. P. Scholfield, Esq.

Sir,—We, the undersigned Commoners of Ibsley Common, should be very much obliged if you would bring the following request before Lord Normanton, namely, that we should be allowed to burn the furze and heath on the parts of the Common called Brogenslade and Leadenhall.

Of late years the furze has very much increased, consequently the feed has diminished, and the danger of unauthorized fires has increased. We believe that such authorized burning, as we are now venturing to propose to his Lordship, would be of great benefit to the feed, and of no damage to the sporting value of the Common, as the portion we indicate is not frequented by game. If, as we hope, his Lordship will favourably consider our request, we would all undertake to assist in the burning, and to keep it within bounds, and would fulfil, to the best of our ability, all such conditions as it may be thought fit to impose. Signed: Heywood Sumner, John Thomas, James Hayter, James Viney, Stephen Shutler, George Thomas, James Thomas, Charles Pope, G. Wickham, A. Wyatt, Alfred Bundy, Samuel Philpott, Henry Bason, T. F. C. Read, James Banks."

In due time we got the following reply:

March 22, 1906.

Gentlemen,

I now write to say that I have seen Lord Normanton with reference to your letter of the 12th instant, and your request as to the burning of certain portions of furze and heath on Ibsley Common.

Lord Normanton is very willing that you should carry out what you suggest, provided every care is taken to keep the burning within proper bounds, and that he is not held responsible for any damage to property. I feel sure that every care will be taken.

Believe me, Gentlemen, your obedient servant, E. P. Scholfield.

So that was settled. Accordingly a convenient day was chosen, and on Saturday, 31st March, we all assembled at 9 o'clock in the morning, and began to set fire to the furze patches along the Hucklesbrook. They behaved just like the furze fires on Gorley Hill. The flames blazed up furiously for a time, and then abruptly died down without spreading; and so each man went about with a burning brand, setting light to the straggling patches of furze. Dorridge was soon hidden by the smoke of innumerable fires. Women with their babies stood watching on the windward side. The children were scared by the crackle and roar of the flames, and really behaved with great caution; while Lizzie Thomas (the deaf mute) made strange inarticulate sounds of warning whenever the fires seemed to be dangerously near to her father's fernrick.

From Furze Hill we burnt our fiery way up Brogenslade, and all went well till we got to the deep-rutted drokes at the top. Here the furze brakes are thickly fringed with heather and sedgegrass, and here we found, to our cost, that we had lit more fires than we could control. A brisk north-wester was now blowing, and the fire began running up the hill and across the plain, followed by a fringe of beaters, too few to stop the fire, but sufficient to keep the running flames within bounds till they reached Ladywell, and here we succeeded in beating them out. By 3 o'clock we could safely leave the charred ground. Although we had burnt more than we intended, still no real damage had been done. So far, so good; and when John Thomas met us on our way home with a can of welcome cider, we could slake our thirsty, smoke-dried throats, feeling well pleased at the success of the first authorized burning of the Common within the memory of man.

Our pleasure was short-lived. At night unauthorized fires were lit, first on Gorley Hill, and then beyond Mockbeggar. The latter was a very big blaze, for

the furze and heath had grown high on the southern side of the hills, and this fire raged furiously from 9 o'clock to the small hours of Sunday morning. The turf-cutters grumbled at the loss of a good turf-ground, while the keepers, wholly disclaiming the fire, approved the result, as it would save them trouble in looking for outlying pheasants' nests.

Then followed a week of warnings and nightly watchings. On Monday morning I heard indirectly that "they" meant to burn the furze on Cuckoo Hill; and in the afternoon, as I was bicycling to Stuckton to tell the policeman to be on the look-out, I was stopped by a friendly upraised arm. Again the same warning: " 'They' are going to burn Cuckoo's Hill to-night." Accordingly the policeman (in plain clothes), Samuel Philpott, Harry Roberts, and I lurked about on the hill until eleven o'clock in the hope of catching "they." But in vain. Distant fires at Godshill and beyond Picked Post lighted up the horizon and kept us on the alert, and from time to time we caught each other, after mutual stalking among the furze brake, but the threat of which I had been warned was not fulfilled.

Throughout the week we continued on the watch, and on most nights there were fires either on Gorley Hill, Rockford Common, Linwood Bog, or across the valley at Plumley. On Sunday night we expected a respite—out of the respect due to Sunday clothes, if not to the day!—but this expectation was not fulfilled: our supper was abruptly interrupted by the announcement that the Common was on fire. And really it did look like the whole Common afire when my son and I ran out of the back door. The rounded hills above Shutler's cottage were fringed with racing flames. Rings of fire were creeping round the eastern sides of Dorridge, while dense clouds of smoke, lit up by flaring sparks, showed that the

Ibsley Common afire. Ap: 8. 1906.

self-sown thickets of little firs had been lighted on the western side of the clump. My son ran up to the fire, armed with a fir-tree beater—of which I had now laid in a stock—while I kept guard on our hill, as with such fires about, I feared lest more might happen nearer home. He was the first to get to the fire that was now burning up on the plain beyond North Hollow gravel-pit, and I soon heard his halloos for help, which were presently answered from Furze Hill. Then Samuel Philpott came along the top of Cuckoo Hill where I was watching, and so I left him in charge with Harry Roberts, who had also appeared, and went up myself to the fire-beating line.

There was a high north-west wind blowing, and the fire had become quite unmanageable. It was impossible to maintain effective beating owing to the gusty wind and to the heat of the creeping, darting, driven flames that rushed up and down the hills with a sinister, flapping roar, while fiery clouds of dense smoke magnified the fire to vast proportions, and reduced our efforts to apparent futility. A few men with fir boughs seemed a very puny opposition to such a raging element. At first we feared for Robin Hood's Clump, and that the fire would come along our hill, but we managed by vigorous beating to keep it above the top end of Great Chibden Bottom, and then, as soon as we got to places where turf cutting had left bare patches, it was possible for our line of eight or ten men to beat out the flames as fast as we could walk. In this way we turned the fire before it reached Newtown and Noyce's cottage, while on the further side of the Common the fire, after skirting Whitefield Clump, burnt itself out on the previous burning of a week before. So, after four hours of incessant beating, with our boughs charred and tattered, with blistered hands and blackened faces, we were able to rest at last, for the fire was finally stopped. At one o'clock on Monday morning we left the Common in darkness.

A strange incident of these fires on Ibsley Common was the running accompaniment of explosions that here and there followed the flames. They were caused by soldiers' cartridges which had been dropped during the manoeuvres of 1898, and which were now discovered by the searching fire, and tested after years of exposure in the moss and heather. We may certainly claim that we keep our powder dry.

Two young men from "up along" were caught lighting furze on Gorley Hill, and they got two months apiece for thus mis-using a matchbox, but the fires on Ibsley Common kept their own secret. Their lighting up was never traced, and remained a matter of dark suspicion, of hints, and of solemn knowing nods among ill-informed heads.

The Common quickly recovered from its blackened state. In three weeks time, green blades were pushing up through the ashes, and the ponies and sheep were nibbling the tender tops of the young sedge-grass. By June, the heather had begun to shoot, the burnt furze to break from the roots, surrounded by innumerable seedlings, and the fern was covering Brogenslade, Great Chibden Bottom, and Whitefield Plain—indeed, these parts of the Common were much greener than heretofore. The charred stems of the furze bushes are the ugliest relics of heath fires; they remain tough, and stand for a year, when they rot at the root, and are then easily broken off either by children for firewood, or by the wandering cattle.

In 1907 Mr. E. P. Scholfield sent round the following notice to the commoners: "A meeting will be held at Gorley School on Friday, the 12th of April, at 7.30 p.m., which all those who have Common rights on Gorley, Ibsley, and Rockford Commons are invited to attend to discuss the question of systematic burning of the heather on these Commons, so as to prevent, if possible, incendiary fires." It was a pouring wet evening when we met, the heavens were evidently blessing our endeavours to prevent incendiary fires. About 30 commoners attended. Mr. Scholfield took the chair, expressed Lord Normanton's interest in the matter, and asked for the opinion of those present as to the best way of organizing yearly burnings on the Commons. James Hayter, John Thomas, Viney, Roberts, and I gave our opinions. It was generally agreed that the burning of selected pieces of the Commons would be a great benefit—that it was now too late for heath burning—that no burning was needed either on Ibsley or Rockford Commons after the great fires of last year, but that a specified tract of furze should be burned as soon as possible on Gorley Common. Eventually I moved, and James Hayter seconded, a resolution to this effect: "It is agreed by this meeting of Gorley, Ibsley, and Rockford commoners that, with permission of the Lord of the Manor, there shall be an annual meeting of the said commoners, in the month of February, to arrange for such burning as may be necessary, and other matters connected with the Commons." This was carried unanimously, and the meeting ended at 8.30, after a vote of thanks to Lord Normanton for calling the meeting, and to Mr. Scholfield for presiding.

On Friday, 19th April, we burnt the tract of furze as authorized at the commoners' meeting: from the top of Buddles to Deacon's cottage, thence up to the race-course path, then across to the gravel pit. It was a still day, and the furze burnt well, but needed much lighting owing to its patchy growth. We began at 10 o'clock and finished at 1 o'clock. The result was apparent by midsummer in the improved feed.

On Monday, 16th March, 1908, we had another authorized burning on Ibsley Common, after a preliminary meeting in February, at the school, which was largely attended by commoners of Ibsley, Gorley and Rockford. In the morning we burnt from the top end of Great Chibden Bottom, across the plain to Leaden Hall, and down the far side hills to Linwood bog, thus dividing the Common by a broad track of burnt ground, so that a heath fire cannot now run from beginning to end of the Common—as it did four years ago. In the afternoon we burnt large tracts of heath and furze on both sides of Chibden Bottom. While we were engaged with our job a hunted buck crossed the Common, coming from Newlands and on his way to Broomy. There was no scent when the hounds came to the recently burnt ground which the buck had crossed.

At the commoners' meeting of 1909 it was decided that no burning was necessary.

The subject of heath fires is naturally a contentious question. In 1908 much burning was done up in the Forest; on the whole, well done, but great was the outcry in the daily press, principally from outside opinion. But the hasty complaints of townspeople who pose as defenders of the Forest do not express the forester's point of view, for he knows and looks ahead; he knows that when furze gets old, the land on which it grows ultimately gets "furze sick," and unless it is renewed by burning, the furze-brakes will gradually perish. He minds old brakes that have thus died down in his lifetime. He knows that the young feed is the best keep for his cattle and ponies, and that anyhow they have to work hard for their living. He knows the danger of a running fire getting into the hollies that skirt the old woods, and he does not forget his winter holly harvest—so the forester has a blind side for burnt tracks that will ensure safety for years from running heath fires, at the expense of ugliness that only lasts for a season.

For feed, burn the bottoms but not the hills. Such is our local opinion. Moreover, burn early in the year, and when the heath is not too dry, otherwise the fire may burn down to the roots, in which case the plants do not recover. The importance of early burning is recognized in Scotland, for heather burning is controlled by an Act passed in 1773, whereby any person setting fire to heath or moor between 11th April and 1st November is, on conviction, liable to a penalty of £2 for the first offence, £5 for the second, and £10 for the third and every subsequent offence, or, failing payment, imprisonment.

Bracken, sedge-grass, mat-grass, and dodder specially flourish after a fire. Dwarf furze spreads quicker than heath on land that has been overburnt or late burnt.

In 1907 some bad work was done on Ocknell Plain, and the fire got into the beautiful old woods at Winding Stonehard, and burnt many hollies and crab-apple trees. With experience, care, and sufficient beaters this should never happen. The way to keep a heath fire in hand is as follows: Burn a stop-track at the down wind end of the piece of heath that is intended to be burnt, thus—first light fires at 1, 2, 3, and 4 (see diagram above), sufficiently near to intersect each other when they have burnt a small fiery circle; thus they will burn themselves out, except at the outsides which must be beaten out. Do not light more of these stop-track fires than your beaters can manage. When the stop-track has been thus burnt, and beaten out, set alight to the up-wind end of the main piece of heath intended to be burnt, which fire can be kept in hand at the sides, while it will burn itself out when it comes to the previously burnt stop-track.

THE BOOK OF GORLEY, 23–9

COTTAGE CHRONICLES

My first visit to the Tames farm at Boldrewood was in the year 1882. Old Tame had been Mr. Duckworth's gardener at Beechwood, and at the time I write of had retired, and was living with his son and daughter-in-law, still able, however, to do regular garden work, and occupying a tiny room and a large four-post bed. He was then an old man of 84, shrewd, wise in his garden craft, ready in speech, and a staunch Dissenter. He lived on into this century, and died at the age of 103.

In the years 1897 and 1899 I had long talks with the old man. He spent time every day in writing texts on slips of paper, which he wrapped carefully round smooth stones, and gave to the keeper's children to be dropped on the road as they went to Minstead or Emery Down. Some one, he said, would pick up the little parcels, would open them and read the papers, and just as David overcame Goliath with a sling and five smooth stones, so his stones, winged with texts, would surely find their billet.

Old Tame had been a Wesleyan preacher, so his talk was naturally reminiscent of his Chapel experience, and the following is a record, taken down at the time, of some of our conversation when the old man was over 100 years of age.

"My eyesight's garn, can't see 'ee, but I've been reading the Bible." "Does B. read to you?" "No" (with a grave chuckle), "the Lard reads to me. He called me away from where the men was a-mowing, when I was 21, beside a girt dog's tomb, and then I knelt down behind that stone, and prayed to the Lard. But I kep secret: so I fell away agen, and live in sin for ten years. I was sitting in the church at Bramshaw, in the old sinful ways, and I was a-looking at the parson and a-thinking, I shan't get much good out of 'ee, when the Lard call me the second time, His vaice comed out o' the wall, 'This is no place for 'ee.' So I know'd I was called for His service, and I comed out o' church, and never been in one since. Yes; I took up with the Wesleyans, and I preached, and so they all took and hated me. In the world 'ee shall have tribulation, and I knew my enemies would try to overthrow me. They kep on saying things to my master agen me. One day I was a-praying agen my enemies, by the hot-water pipes in the greenhouse, and the Lard heard me, and He took me up from behind, so I knew that I was in the hand of the Lard; and when I come out, my master he comed to me and says, 'Tame, I'm a-going away for a bit; here's £5 for 'ee to pay the wages, and for to keep 'ee going while I'm away.' And so my enemies was all confounded, and so they always have a-been." Then he went on multiplying stories of his enemies, showing how tiresome and wicked they had been, and how continually they had been confounded. When I had an opportunity, I tried to change the subject by saying that I was staying at Bournemouth, and had ridden over on my bicycle, at which he sharply rapped out, "Another of the works of the Devil," and fresh fuel was added to his fiery anathemas on the wiles of the wicked. So my plan failed.

Old Tame died in 1900, and his strong character and great age have made him memorable in this countryside. He was a point of interest in the Forest—like one of the most ancient trees—and stories are "minded" of the old man's sayings and doings. When he was 100, he was dissatisfied with some boots that were made for him at Lyndhurst—they were too thin—so he went to complain. The bootmaker retaliated: "They're thick enough for any walking you'll want," to which old Tame replied: "Well, I've begun my second 100 a good sight stronger than I did my first."

THE BOOK OF GORLEY, 30–1

POMONA

"The Book of the Apple" thus gives the Saxon Coronation Benediction: "Bless, O Lord, the courage of this Prince, and prosper the work of his hands; and by Thy blessing may this land be filled with Apples, with the fruit and dew of heaven, from the top of the ancient mountains, from the Apples of the eternal hills, from the fruits of the earth and its fulness." So, when our trees are covered with apples in the autumn, and the laden branches are trigged up to bear their burden, and the orchard grass is spotted with fallen fruit, the blessing of a thousand years ago is still received in the ruddy gift of Pomona. Yet, I must confess, this tribute comes from an unworthy worshipper! Alas, I cannot eat an apple. No; my pleasure is vicarious. I grow apples for others to eat, and praise the goddess untasted. Still, my love of apples is not wholly platonic. Though Eve may no longer tempt me, Noah does, and good cider is to my taste the best of all our native drinks. The amber juice is pressed from the heart of a hundred sunny days; it recalls sights and scents of the orchard's wealth, and the keen, mellow draught comes from the bountiful breasts of the very goddess herself—Pomona. But, remember, there is cider and cider. I do not write the praises of the usual commercial beverage—of bottled cider, of sparkling cider, of "our native champagne." My best cider is pure apple-juice, fermented, without any addition, and fresh drawn from the cask.

In cider-making the first consideration must be given to the apples. You must not expect to get a good result from a heap of rotting windfalls. The apples that we mostly use for cider are the common apples of our countryside, namely, Codlings, Pearmains, Orange Pippins, Profits, and Davys. The best combination I have yet to learn: and I have planted Red-streaks, Kingston-Black, Morgan's-Sweet, Foxwhelp, Wine-sour, and Bitter-sweets to further this purpose. Where the apple trees grow must also be taken into consideration. The apples should come from good, strong land, for the fruit of apple trees growing on a gravelly soil makes a white and watery cider. Our apples and Furze Hill apples make good cider, while Ibsley apples make bad cider, owing to the soil, for Ibsley stands on a bed of washed-down valley gravel. Besides the apples, consider the cask. An old spirit, port, or sherry cask is the best. Avoid any other. Cider in an old cider cask is not so good as cider in a new spirit, port, or sherry cask. By "new" I mean new to cider as its contents.

Now for the making. Apples ruddy, golden, and green lie around in heaps. Slabs of pomace, speckled, brown, and yellow, tell of the cider-press. The same tale is told by the faint, pervading smell of sweet malic juice which is being squeezed from the crushed fruit. The cider-makers grind the apples and work the

The Apple Mill

press, and ladle the brown liquor from the receiving tubs into the casks till their long sacking aprons are splashed with signs of every stage of the making—rind, pips, apple-juice, pomace—and so they win the gift of Pomona.

The apple-mill, the cider-press, the tubs, the peck, and the casks are the necessary plant for this job of cider-making. They must all be as clean as hard scrubbing can make them. First, the trough of the apple-mill is filled with a sack of apples, then two men work the handles of the wheel, and the heap of apples in the trough quickly sinks through the slicing cogs of the hand-mill, and fall as pulp into the receiving tub. Then this pulp is shovelled into a rough horsehair cloth, neatly folded, and the package is put into the press. Seven times is this shovelling and folding repeated with seven cloths, and with the seventh of such packings of

The Press

pulp the press is full. The top is then put on, and the press screws are lowered by two men who work them by means of wooden winches on either side of the press. As the pressure increases, the apple-juice begins to flow from a vent-hole at the bottom of the press, and is caught by a receiving tub. Then, after the last turn of the screws has been exacted by the short two-handed wooden winches, a long four-handed iron winch is used and further last turns are slowly obtained from the reluctant screws, till at length no more can be got, and the press is left to drain off the final drippings of the expressed juice. Now another sack of apples is reduced to pulp by the grinder. Then the men return to the squeezed-out press. It is unscrewed, and the first lot of pulp is taken out and put back in the now empty trough of the apple-mill. Again the men return to the press; the pulp of the second sack of apples is wrapped according to the same method in the horsehair cloths, and pressed in the same manner as the first. Then, on completion, the second lot of pulp is taken out of the press, put in the trough with the first lot, and both are ground together for the second time, and afterwards both lots (now ground and pressed into half their first compass) are put into the press together and pressed for the second time. Thus every drop of juice is squeezed and crushed from the pulp which has by this time been compressed into slabs of brown pomace—only fit for pig food.

The liquor that runs from the press into the receiving tub is of a muddy golden colour; the darker it is, the better hopes have the cider-makers of the future quality of the cider. When the receiving tub is full, it is carried to the cask, and its contents are baled out in the peck, then poured on the head of the cask, whence the liquor runs into the cask through the bung-hole.

Two sacks of apples make about 22 to 24 gallons of cider. The horsehair cloths are needed to strain off the pips and pulp which otherwise would find their way into the liquor. These cloths cost 7*s.* 6*d.* each, and only last about two years. They shrink considerably under their usage. When the cask is filled, it is carted away to its destination, and is there put away in a cool place to ferment. This fermentation goes on for about a fortnight or three weeks, during which time the top of the cask-head is covered with the cider froth that rises up through the open bung-hole with a soft hissing sound. Gradually this ceases, the froth subsides, the bung may then be driven in, and the cider must now be left to clear. In six weeks it will be good to drink, but will not be clear and bright for three or four months.

Such is the way that cider is made here—apple-juice, pure and simple—and, the result being very good, of course cunning housewives think to improve on it by dodges—for example, by adding pricked raisins, cloves, or sugar before the cider has finished fermenting. Then they dignify the drink with the name of "cider-wine"; but I do not like it. As I have said, my best cider is pure apple-juice, fermented, without any addition, and kept in a cask on draught. But remember that cider thus made should be drunk within a year, or it will get "hard." If you want it to keep longer, you must add some sugar.

THE BOOK OF GORLEY, 48–51

A WINTER WALK IN THE NEW FOREST

61

Winter has its own especial charm for perambulation in the Forest. The bare, deciduous trees reveal exquisite tracery of branch and twig, surmounted by a veil of varied tinted buds. Green mosses of vivid hues mingle with the grey fur of lichens on bole and trunk and bough. Far vistas open out through woodland withered undergrowth, and (blessed exemption) there are no flies to torment the pilgrim.

The Northern side of the Forest adjoins my home, and here, as they say of ghosts, I walk—alone for preference, when bent on hide-and-seek, that is to say, seeking for ancient sites hidden in the soil. I like the absolute freedom of being alone when I am fossicking about for uncertain discovery of this or that; one is more free to turn aside, haver, seek and fail to find, yet to return home not wholly dissatisfied, because such negative results will be of future value in narrowing the area to be searched. "Thank the Lord for solitude" is my grace before walk, to-day, when I want to locate and to estimate some Forest sites of which I have been informed. One, a small, oval enclosure at the Eastern end of Pinnick. The others, doubtful, near Rakes Brakes Bottom.

Accordingly I cross Ibsley Common, which is a detached ridge and plain of plateau gravel rising 257 feet above the sea, and stretching from Mockbeggar to Ogden's Purlieu; descend to Digden bog, snipe-haunted; across Ill bridge spanning Docken's water with sawn-log treads; up through holly thickets to the Eastern corner of Appleslade; then downhill through the old oaks and glades of Redshoot to Greenford Bottom, where the brook meanders down an open, waterlogged valley towards Linford; then uphill over boggy slopes, and through dense thickets, wherein grow strange old holly trees, pollarded and re-grown with fantastic variations; on and up, until the boggy ground ceases at the foot of an abrupt ramp, above which is firm ground with better growth. Near here is the first sought-for site. Here, or hereabouts. Now the *dramatis persona* goes very slow—questing, and questing, across the woodland floor of fallen leaves, windfall branches, brambles and fern stubble beneath a crowd of oaks until, at length, a low continuous rise on the woodland floor is spotted, and a small oval enclosure found (20 paces long by 16 paces wide), with a long pace-wide gap entrance on the South side above Akercombe Bottom; surrounded by a wasted bank about 1 foot 6 inches high above a silted-up outside ditch, measuring 15 feet over-all. This little earthwork is unrecorded, until now; its discovery is owing to information received from Mrs. T. G. Longstaff and her family on picnic bent.

And here I lout and apologize for intrusion, the said family believe—nay, they know that this enclosure is a fairy ring; they must never read the prosaic attribution following.

On the Western bank of the enclosure an old oak and a holly tree grow, self-sown, that suggest a vague anterior date for the enclosure. These trees can scarcely be less than 300 years old.

They must have been allowed to grow after this enclosure had been made—as I

The Fairy Ring Pound in Pinnick – restored & explained.

think it was—for a pannage-feeding pig-pound. It is too large, too far from habitation, and too consolidated in its earthwork for a bee-garden. If it was used as a pig-pound we may restore it in our mind's eye with a "hedge," *i.e.*, stockade on the top of the surrounding bank, of which the slight elevation and over-all measurement suggest keeping in stock, not keeping out wolves, as its purpose. J. E. Harting considers that wolves became extinct in England in the time of Henry VII, 1485–1509—which perhaps gives us another clue to an approximate date for the site, *i.e.*, not much earlier than the sixteenth century.

In William Gilpin's *Remarks on Forest Scenery*, 1st edition, 1794, vol. ii, p. 112, *et seq.*, there is an interesting account of the methods by which a forest swineherd reduced his pannage-feeding pigs to perfect obedience—methods perhaps traditional, as suggested in my illustration. Thus, the swineherd made a little pound, with fenced shelter around, and fern bedding afloor, and then collected all the acorns he could find, and laid them in heaps within the pound. Then, in the evening, sounding his horn, he drove his pigs into the pound where they found (without seeking) heaps of acorns and comfortable bedding. Next evening the swineherd again blew his horn, but his pigs no longer required to be driven, they obeyed his summons, they associated the sound of the horn with acorns galore and comfy bedding, and thus the habit of returning to the pound every evening became impressed on pig minds.

Probably Medieval, is my inscription for this earthwork. Why? May not these self-sown trees have grown on a derelict Roman or British earthwork? Why Medieval?

Because the over-all measurements of comparable Roman or British earthworks are always larger than this.

Because the over-all measurement of this earthwork compares with those of Medieval "encoppicement" examples at Ridley and Old Sloden.

Because the bank of this earthwork is only semi-consolidated with the adjacent soil; ancient earthworks belonging to the earlier periods aforesaid are wholly consolidated.

The site was well chosen, on a spur of plateau gravel outlying the Handy Cross Pond ridge, facing South, with water near by in Akercombe Bottom, which latter name testifies to this place having been noted for plenty of acorn pannage "time along."

New Forest soil has advantages and disadvantages, amongst the latter an excavator must include the bone-destroying acids that percolate through its soil. Excepting burnt bones, no bones are found on ancient sites here, so we have no knowledge of cattle or pigs kept by our New Forest forefathers, and only pony shoes (found on the Pottery sites) to indicate the small size of Romano-British ponies. On the chalk of Cranborne Chase, 12 miles distant, bones are fairly well preserved in the sub-soil. We do know from General Pitt-Rivers' excavations there, on Romano-British sites, that their pigs were taller at the shoulder but shorter in the back than our cross-bred pig, and that they retained many of the wild-boar characteristics; but there is a great gap between the end of the fourth century A.D. and Medieval times, only partially bridged by scribal illustration, wherein the pigs delineated seem still to comply with such type of high-shouldered rather short-backed pig.

My next point is Holly Hatch, about 3 miles distant, where stands a lone keeper's cottage, near which are the other two sites that I want to investigate. My way goes through Roe Wood Inclosure; along the ride running South to North that crosses the broad consolidated entrenchments of a small camp, called Castle Piece, belonging to the class of pre-Roman earthworks that Dr. J. P. Williams-Freeman names "Woodland Ringworks"; across the track from Roe cottage to Bratley; through the cut clearances of Scots pine in Milkham Inclosure, and out into the open expanse of Broomy Plain, whence there is a glorious prospect over Cranborne Chase, and the district to the West and North-West where three counties meet, namely, Hants, Wilts, and Dorset.

So far, through all these woodland solitudes, not a single deer has been seen, where, only a few years ago deer would have been seen in numbers. I have seen a herd of 29 deer in Greenford Bottom, and have seen and heard a bellowing stag

RD'S EYE VIEW OF BADBURY RINGS LOOKING SOUTH · Watercolour, 1914, 44.4 × 66.6cm

EXCAVATIONS AT ROCKBOURNE DOWN · Watercolour, 1912, 17.5 × 31cm

A GLADE IN THE NEW FOREST · Watercolour, 13.7 × 34.7cm

NEW FOREST VIEW · Watercolour, 38.4 × 60.7cm

MSTEAD AT NEWTOWN · Watercolour, 1905, 33 × 63.3cm

EP SHEARING · Watercolour, 29.7 × 44cm

CUCKOO HILL AND THE VALLEY OF THE AVON · Pen, ink and watercolour, from sketchbook, 1910–11, 8.5 ×

ES IN THE NEW FOREST · Pen, ink and watercolour, from sketchbook, 1904, 11.5 × 34.5cm

DANEBURY HILL FROM BROUGHTON · Pen, ink and watercolour, from sketchbook, about 1895, 12.5 × 17.5cm

with attendant hinds in the rutting season, ringing round and round through underwood near Castle Piece, and the following tale of "Veiw of Deere," here, in 1908, will further show the difference in this respect between then and now. My son Humphrey, and I, were walking home from Greenford, after a morning spent in watching the deer-hounds hunting around Pinnick, Redshoot, Roe and Milkham; we returned through Appleslade, on the chance of seeing some of the disturbed deer—as we did—four does got up, and preceded us through the wood; then, as we crossed Rockford Common, we spied a buck, near Paddy Bussy's firs, who leisurely disappeared over the brow of the hill, we following, to be rewarded by a view of five bucks, all standing at gaze on the top of a little knap in Roden's Bottom. They regarded our advent with unconcern, and only after they had fulfilled their curiosity moved from the knap towards the Linwood road. We were evidently set down as harmless. My son then went to the left, I to the right—both of us now unseen by the deer—with intention to drive them off Rockford on to Ibsley Common, in which we were successful, for when we emerged in view, they stotted off across the heather and sweet-gale in Digden Bottom, crossed Docken's water rather reluctantly, then paused in the further bog, and again stood at gaze; my son then made for Newlands bridge, while the bucks and I watched each other. After a time they turned, picked their way across the bog, and went up the hill towards Newlands; here they were headed by my son, who, at the same time, put up three does who were lying in the heather, and then the little herd of eight deer crossed Whitefield Plain, to the great surprise of the commoners' ponies, one of which reared violently and repeatedly, shaking his shackled fore-legs at the intruders, but the deer took no heed, and trotted on to the top of Little Chibden Bottom. Here they stopped, and again stood at gaze. Now, our project was to head them into Great Chibden Bottom towards Cuckoo Hill. But this was too much. The bucks seemed to decide that they had been playing long enough with us, and trotted straight away, followed by cantering does, across the plain to Leadenhall, down Ladywell Droke, and thence out of sight, despite our desperate efforts to head them. Thus ended our private "Veiw of Deere in the New fforest," 20th January 1908, while mine, 9th December 1924, had (so far) resulted in not a single deer having been seen. It should be noted that such decrease in the New Forest deer is not due to adverse natural conditions, but to buckshot, the deer being now shot down to a prescribed limit in number.

Well, after this reminiscent halt by the way, I must get on over the plain; past Broomy Lodge; then downhill through Broomy Inclosure, with oak canopy above and fern undergrowth; then, as open daylight beyond the track distance begins to foretell the end of the wood, cock-crow and dog-bark tell that habitation is nigh. Holly Hatch cottage to wit, standing trim and homely beside the way from Broomy to Fritham, on the Northern verge of the Inclosure. It radiates well-being, and a high standard of up-keep, maintaining lonely credit to both Crown and keeper.

"A mound that rises above the bracken undergrowth of Holly Hatch, on the left hand side of the bottom ride before you come to the hollies," is my direction for the first supposed site here; that leads me without check to the spot. A mound riddled by rabbits and their scrapes, the up-turn of which proclaims at once its natural origin. This mound is one of many scattered over this district of Eocene formation, where predominant sand in a soil patch lying amid surrounding clay has retarded its denudation beneath the elements, for clay denudes more rapidly than sand. Sometimes these sand hillocks assume the appearance of a barrow, for example, "Black Barrow" and "Purlieu Pound," lower down in the Docken's valley; sometimes of continuous scarps or ramps, for example, in Eyeworth Wood, where such natural formations misled J. R. Wise (*The New Forest*, p. 222) when he wrote: "On the North-east side of the wood are the remains of a fine Roman camp, the agger and vallum being in one place nearly complete." Again, on the Western side of "Pipers Weight," and around "Lucas Castle," may be found such continuous scarps or ramps that are formed by natural causes, *i.e.*, soil as affected by subaerial denudation. *Ex uno disce omnes*, I forbear multiplying examples. They are many throughout this district.

"Outside Old Sloden, above Rakes Brakes Bottom, there is a rabbit bury with black earth up-turned." Such is my further direction for the second of the supposed sites near here: if the up-turn had included potsherds, I should have had better hope of finding an unrecorded Roman kiln site, but, notwithstanding, it is a likely place, as there is a Roman kiln site close by inside Old Sloden, which I excavated in 1920. So with hope, and caution, I skirt round the boggy edges of the bottom up to the hillside crowned by old trees.

Here, at length, I have a present-day "Veiw of Deere"—four bucks lying just outside the wood beside some holly trees. We go through the usual ritual. *Dramatis persona* stock still. Deer disturbed, at gaze, curious and undecided, but eventually moving off to a further distance, then stopping and again looking back at the stock-still figure, when suddenly they come to a conclusion, and spring across the brake into the fringe of thickets beside the bog, leaving a sense of vacancy in the forest scene when they have gone.

On going up to the place where the bucks were lying, the soft soil bears the impress of where they lay; close by are rabbit-holes, and grey-black sandy scrapes, behold the very place for which I was seeking—"a rabbit bury with black earth up-turned outside Old Sloden"; but, alas, inspection shows that the scrapes are of natural grey-black sandy soil mixed with pebblestones, not of greasy black soil mixed with potsherds; and, again, I have to add to my list of searches in vain. This grey-black sandy soil occurs in patches throughout the Forest, and the colour seems to be due to the occasional black humus of the top soil. The black relics of decay are often difficult to differentiate from those of burnt stuff.

With one hit and two misses as my record to-day, I plod up to the top of the hill in order to see how Fritham Plain has recovered from the heath fires of recent years, when many fine outlying hollies were burnt here, besides old furze brakes. Furze that has been thus burnt, generally shoots at the root in a year's time. Not so old furze brakes—which are sometimes finally destroyed by a fire—perhaps because through long occupancy their landpatch has become "furze-sick"—a foresters' term for land-patches on which furze brakes have died of old age, without subsequent renewal by natural regeneration. The black desolation left by such fires is a dismal sight, and the damage done seems to be irreparable, but the holly stools generally survive notwithstanding; their trunks and charred boughs will be cut and sold for fuel; then, in a few years, young holly shoots will be springing up around blackened stools, and in time there will again be holly bushes crowded with glistening foliage and coral berries. Not so with Scots pine, if their foliage is burnt, or even scorched, they are done for; they never try again. They die, sulking.

Such come-by-mischance fuel is bought from the Crown by adjacent foresters, who supply local demand for firewood. Many loads of this charred holly-wood have kept my home fires burning for the last three years. When sapless and thoroughly dry, holly-wood is fine fuel; it is very close in grain, burns evenly, and gives out great heat; but, unlike ash-wood fuel, it is not fit for burning at once, whereas ash may be cut to-day, and will give a blazing fire to-morrow. Oak, like holly, needs keeping for two or three years before burning. Elm burns badly at any time, gives out little heat, and smells unpleasantly in the wood-basket. Scots pine varies, it may be good or it may be bad, it may spit sparks and splutter; but either way it leaves hardly any ash after its logs have been consumed; a dual objection, for a hot core of wood-ash in the grate warms the room all night, and speeds fire renewal in the morning—while in spring when pine ash cores are removed for manure, the gardener grumbles at his small benefit received! The only cedar that I have burnt, spluttered and popped in an agitating manner, but had a most pleasant smell. Apple-wood also is sweet-smelling when burnt, but needs long keeping before burning.

Such is my experience of wood fuel, burnt here during twenty-eight years past—wherein naught else has been burnt in our grates—except in the kitchen.

And now my steps turn homewards, along the wooded ridge of Old Sloden; over minor earthworks which I have described and illustrated in *The Ancient*

Small Square Enclosure on Sloden Hill . H.S. 1913.

Earthworks of the New Forest; down the steep Western bluff; across the open heath towards Hasley, where the track mounts and descends a sandy knoll; here it has been curiously channelled by the recent heavy rain (1.47 inches fell on 15th December 1924). The track is aligned on each side by sandy banks, now indented by drumming raindrops into a mottled grey surface, while down the track the rushing rainwater had deposited a smooth white course of washed silver-sand, current-bedded, with marks of miniature swirls and eddies scored on its surface, crisp and fresh, as though chased by a fluent tool. It was really too beautiful to be trodden underfoot.

On, beyond, on the Northern side of Hasley Inclosure, there is another sandy knoll of which the sand is bright orange in colour, containing fragments of ironstone limonite, a concretionary natural product of sand indurated with iron, which sometimes forms around roots in the subsoil, and when in time such roots have decayed and wasted away, ironstone tubes remain to provoke question.

Near here, outside the Eastern end of Hasley Inclosure, there are extensive remains of rambling pits and hollows with up-turned mounds adjoining, that may have been made for obtaining ironstone, or heathstone as it is locally called; a stone that was evidently valued by the Romans, for it is constantly found on Roman sites throughout this part of Britain. They used it for the cheeks of hypocaust and kiln furnaces, and for the lining of flues exposed to great heat, because it does not splinter under such conditions; it burns from orange-brown to wine-red under the action of continuous fire. Similar, though lesser, pit diggings may be found on other hilltops near here, notably on the summit of a sugar-loaf hill that rises above Purlieu Pound bog in Ogden's Purlieu, and at "Pits" on Ibsley

Common, where we know that these diggings date back, at least, to Medieval times by the name given to this place in New Forest Perambulations of Edward I, "Putts in Merkynggeslade," and of Charles II, "The Pits," and infer that heathstone was the material sought for, by present-day experience that this stone may still be found here.

Such sites as these are both intriguing and baffling to one who trusts excavation to provide documents—things that teach. There are no indications anywhere among these humps and hollows to direct the excavator's spade; yet there must be chance castaway relics buried beneath these great widespread diggings that would tell us when, and by whom, they were originally made. Ah! if only one had mole sense! An excavator, nowadays, is only half-equipped for his job. He has only two senses that help him, namely, sight, sharpened by experience, and feel, at the end of his delving prong tines; but he has lost the sense that guides the burrowing mole. "Old mole! canst work i' th' earth so fast?" He receives no wireless subterranean messages as does the mole—such sense is atrophied in him by disuse—as is the sense of sight in old mole.

This atrophy of a sense by disuse—one that is not required for livelihood—may be comparatively gauged by considering our sense of smell, and a mole's sense of sight.

We do not depend on our sense of smell in order to procure livelihood. Indeed, if we entirely lost this sense we should not be crippled in dealing with daily life. We should be in danger of undetected gas escapes, but otherwise, if we lived in town, we should perhaps gain, in being immune from street smells; if we lived in country we certainly should lose stray pleasures of scent, year in and year out, but our livelihood would not be threatened. Result: our sense of smell is atrophied.

A mole neither uses nor depends on sight in order to procure his livelihood. He lives in darkness, and, though he has eyes, they are so small, hidden in fur, and unused, that his sense of sight does not convey more than apprehension of daylight as opposed to darkness. He depends solely upon his reception and understanding of wireless subterranean messages for his livelihood, coupled, I should suppose, with an acute sense of feel. Result: a mole's sense of sight is atrophied.

Now compare our sense of sight, on which we have depended for livelihood for countless centuries, with that of a mole. Our sight that ranges from scanning the far horizon to reading small print, and that guides our hands and feet, and informs our minds, all day long, day by day, far and near. If a mole could think, and could appreciate the far-reaching gifts that our sight confers (and which it has lost), might not such thoughtful mole claim for balance against this loss his own far-reaching equipment in the sense and appreciation of smell?

As our sense of sight is—compared with that of a mole; so is a mole's sense of smell—compared with ours.

Such comparison suggests a surrounding subterranean distance charged with wireless messages, directions and calls which we do not apprehend, but which a mole does, and which guide him in procuring his livelihood.

Now this mole sense—this apprehension of subterranean messages—and their interpretation, is the sense that an excavator always longs for.

If only he could receive and interpret faint messages from long-buried relics! Whining below ground around their forgotten graves! Thin, wailing cries—"Save! O Save! we are here—here—and here—and have been buried for centuries, do bring us to the light of day, and we shall help to re-create the Past."

But their S.O.S. is not received—though, maybe, ever repeated, yet certainly never heard.

I wonder! Excavation is a young science, and excavators (despite appearances) must share the attribute. When this science, and those who try to serve it are older, who knows? Such servitors may then be learning to receive and to apprehend messages that now pass by unreceived, unapprehended. I wonder!

Thus musing and walking in undisturbed reverie for two long miles, the *dramatis persona* skirts Hasley Inclosure, crosses the wasting gullies of Ogden's Purlieu, and mounts the plain of Ibsley Common, that is now transfigured by the brief radiance of a wintry sunset. Then descends the green trackway leading down to the Avon valley, to cultivation, and to Cuckoo Hill, in time for tea, with "Thank the Lord for company"—in anticipation, as grace after walk.

PROCEEDINGS OF THE HAMPSHIRE FIELD CLUB AND ARCHAEOLOGICAL SOCIETY, ix, 361–9; reprinted in LOCAL PAPERS, 179–194

IN QUEST OF EARTHWORKS

SUMNER THE TOPOGRAPHER

In 1906 the Committee on Ancient Earthworks and Fortified Enclosures published a report in which it was suggested that all earthworks in Britain should be surveyed with plans drawn up on the 25-inch Ordnance Survey map base. The idea appealed to Sumner and with enormous energy he set about his task. His method was straightforward:

> First, to make a tracing of the 25 inch Ordnance Survey sheet that delineates the earthwork under examination. Then, to study the 6 inch Ordnance Survey sheet of the same place, in order to note the rise and fall of the land by contour lines—which are omitted in the 25 inch scale. Then to examine the site with both the tracing and the 6 inch sheet, in many cases frequently so as to verify the record and to supplement omissions. And finally, to measure up sections of such banks and ditches belonging to the earthwork under examination, as might seem to be typical.
>
> THE ANCIENT EARTHWORKS OF CRANBORNE CHASE, v–vi

In this way he began to plan the earthworks of Cranborne Chase in the spring of 1911.

> Cranborne Chase is a peculiar district. It lies apart from railroads, and apart from most of the road traffic that passes through Ringwood or Salisbury. It is a solitary tract of down-land, corn-land, wood-land, and waste. Dry valleys run far up into the steep flanks of the chalk ridge that is the backbone of the Chase. Streams emerge with intermittent flow in the lower slopes of these valleys.
>
> THE ANCIENT EARTHWORKS OF CRANBORNE CHASE, 5

It was on his doorstep, just across the Avon from Cuckoo Hill. He began in May 1911 with a survey of Grims Ditch and continued for thirteen months, surveying a minimum of one site each month rising to a maximum of six in September 1911. A few more were added in the autumn and winter of 1912–13 and later in 1913 the entire collection was presented as *The Ancient Earthworks of Cranborne Chase*, published by the Chiswick Press in a beautifully illustrated volume (in a limited edition of 200). Our selection below is sufficient to give the reader an indication of the love and care that went into the production. The descriptive sections are perceptive and accurate, while the illustrations—works of art in their own right—provide precise delineation of the earthworks and their environments of a quality that has yet to be surpassed.

Immediately Cranborne Chase was finished Sumner turned his attention to the New Forest and in 1917 produced a companion volume, *The Ancient Earthworks of the New Forest.* Together the two volumes set new standards of illustration which were admired and copied throughout the archaeological world.

During this period of intense survey Sumner developed friendships with two of the great figures of field archaeology—J. P. Williams-Freeman, a doctor who lived and worked near Andover, and O. G. S. Crawford, who was later to run the archaeological division of the Ordnance Survey and become editor of *Antiquity*. Both men were regular guests at Cuckoo Hill over a period of more than twenty years, their visits, for the most part, being timed to coincide with the non-growing season (September to March) when, no doubt, their host would take them on field expeditions to seek earthworks, best seen while the vegetation was low. It may well have been this early contact with Sumner that inspired both men to become leading field archaeologists. In 1915 Williams-Freeman published his, justly famous, book, *An Introduction to Field Archaeology as illustrated by Hampshire*. Although there was a considerable overlap with Sumner's work there was no rivalry and the two men remained close friends throughout the rest of their lives.

In 1918 Sumner was drawn into the ambit of the Bournemouth Natural Science Society, a polymathic association of keen local amateurs, and soon established himself as the principal (and indeed only) archaeologist. In December 1918 he undertook to make a survey of the earthworks in the Bournemouth district, in partnership with W. G. Wallace (son of the famous naturalist who wrote the original paper on natural selection with Darwin). In April of the next year, 1919, they reported verbally on their progress and in 1921 their paper 'Ancient Earthworks of the Bournemouth District' was published in the Society's Proceedings. As a follow up to their survey Wallace undertook a somewhat desultory excavation on the earthworks at St. Catherine's Hill, Christchurch, while Sumner dug a few trenches into the Iron Age fort of Dudsbury.

In the three surveys—Cranborne Chase, the New Forest, and the Bournemouth District—Sumner had covered a very considerable part of Wessex, a block of land some 40 miles east-west and 30 miles north-south, with a degree of thoroughness that left little more to be done and his Map, published in 1923, graphically summed up his achievements. He never lost interest in earthworks, however, and in 1925 in the gently evocative paper 'A Winter Walk in the New Forest' we glimpse the ageing antiquary still hunting for the minor earthworks that had hitherto escaped him—and finding some with evident delight.

EARTHWORKS OF CRANBORNE CHASE

The ruined Buildings of Ancient History either stand near present habitation, or in situations that still appeal to us as being desirable. Roman walls and gateways survive within our towns; Mediaeval Castles dominate modern streets; and Monastic Buildings stand in sheltered valleys bearing witness to a choice that we still endorse. But when we gaze farther back, farther up the stream of time, and when we seek for the relics left by prehistoric men, we find ourselves in places where solitude now reigns. Their camps, their settlements, their cultivation banks, and their boundary ditches were on the hills, remote from present habitation, for the sites which they sought have long since been abandoned. Life has receded from the hill-tops.

Once upon a time great white banks and mounds of upturned chalk crowned our hills, proclaiming the camps of tribal safety, and the tombs of the mighty dead—while lesser white banks rambled up and down the open country, and steep scarps lined the hill-sides, proclaiming pastoral boundaries and primitive cultivation. Then, safety lay on the hill-top. Then, the valleys were shunned, probably because they were swamps and wolf-haunted. But we have abandoned the choice of prehistoric men. Now, down in the fertile valley, shrouded in smoke, lies the modern town, while the rush of the train, and the hoot of the motor tell where our traffic passes. No one seeks the old sites nowadays—except shepherds and their flocks, or sportsmen, or pilgrims in search of the past.

Ichabod may seem to be written on ruined buildings, for they testify to a glory that is departed, but the grassy mounds, and ditches, and hollows of prehistoric sites strike a deeper note of desolation. Here the labours of our forefathers have reverted to Mother Earth, to wild nature, and to the elemental ministry of the seasons.

It is difficult to express the genius of such places, or the dim sense of communication and realization which they impart. Mere proximity, contact, counts for something, however, although it may elude words. The following story expresses this ideal claim. Robert Browning was in Paris with his son, then a little boy, and in some public place pointed out an old gentleman sitting on a seat—"Go up and touch him"—the boy obeyed; when he came back his father said, "Now, when you are a man, remember that to-day you have touched Béranger"—Virtue may go out even to those who only touch the hem of a garment. So Places as well as Persons may impart something to your touch, and it is this reverent touch, inspired by admiration, that I wish to bring to these derelict places that once were inhabited by prehistoric men. This is my purpose. I want to take my reader a far journey across the chalk uplands of Cranborne Chase, in which we may revive the wonder of this primitive life—so remote from our own; and in which we may widen our outlook on familiar scenes as we seek the origins of our present landmarks.

In these days it is possible to look far afield, and to know wide stretches of country, in a manner that was almost impossible to our more rooted forefathers. Formerly, only the horseman could go where we are going; but a horse is a tiresome servant while you wait, and must always be the first care of his rider. We shall do better to depend on our own legs, and on our own seven league boots. What bliss it was in childhood to read of the magical seven league boots, and to see their possessor, in Cruikshank's etching, striding across a landscape! What a gift of the gods, such power of locomotion! What a fantastical conception! And lo, since our childhood, the fairy tale has become fact—common fact so far as concerns our power over seven leagues; for *wheels* were meant though *boots* were written; far and near have changed their relative meaning; every blacksmith in the remotest hamlet can restore our stride if mischance befalls, and so, on silent wheels we can now range far and wide across the country. A bicycle is our magic of seven leagues. It carries us where we will, and then, laid on the grass, it waits our further will. A few drops of oil and our own muscles are its sole demand, while in return it endows us with the magical power of the old fairy tale.

Thus equipped, let us range the chalk summits of Cranborne Chase in quest of earthworks, and our wandering survey will show where lay the prehistoric sites of safety, and the pastoral lands of remote antiquity, and the origins of cultivation. From these we may learn something of the compelling circumstances that shaped life in this unrecorded period, and of the meaning of the humps, and hollows, and dykes, and ditches upon the downs, and we shall gain a new respect for these forsaken earthworks that were wrought by the flint tools, the horn picks, and the patient cunning of our forefathers.

At the outset I would offer a tribute of admiration to the great work done by General Pitt-Rivers, and to its record contained in the four volumes of his *Excavations in Cranborne Chase.* He set a standard that is pre-eminent in its many-sided excellence, and he brought to bear upon his subject a wide experience of primitive antiquities, a genius for the study of origins, and an understanding of the nature of things, that resulted in these invaluable works. They are monuments of original research, and of exact record.

Earthworks can only be really understood by spade-work. The finds may be few, and of a cast-away description, but notwithstanding, they are positive in their evidence, and it is from excavations in the first place that we can increase our knowledge of prehistoric life. We all desire wishing caps, and if mine is ever fitted, I shall wish for another archaeological landowner who shall dig for further knowledge on Cranborne Chase. There is so much to be done. So many questions that are suggested by a superficial survey, and that only excavation can answer. However, excavation has to be regarded as a counsel of perfection, for it cannot cover the field—the earthworks are too numerous—and thus a survey of the varied earthworks on Cranborne Chase may be of help in their interpretation, and of value as a record of landmarks that are always liable to destruction. For destruction is what happens under cultivation. Ancient banks are spread and ditches filled in, till gradually a low rise and fall in the land is all that remains as the present witness of a past site. In some cases the obliteration is complete. Everywhere the plough has been at work destroying these earthen marks of prehistoric men. The Farmer cannot be expected to pay rent on behalf of the Archaeologist, and entrenched sites have generally been regarded merely as humpy ground. When Dr. Stukeley, in 1723, explored the Roman Road from Old Sarum to Winchester, he chanced upon a sample of this destruction—"This way passes the river Bourn at Ford: the ridge of it is plain, though the countrymen has attacked it vigorously on both sides with their ploughs: we caught them at their sacrilegious work, and reprehended them for it." Poor countrymen, scolded by archaeologists, ignored by legislators, but well remembered by the tax-collector. The Archaeologist who catches them at their sacrilegious work, and reprehends them for it, forgets the rent, the risks, and the difficult livelihood of the countryman. The burden of the preservation of ancient earthworks needs to be placed on broader shoulders than those that have hitherto chanced to bear them. Really, we owe some gratitude to the peaceful cultivator for the fragments that remain.

Still, the loss is deplorable that we have suffered through these vigorous attacks of the countryman. This loss has come from lack of national imagination. If we had realized the meaning of these useless earthworks they would have been preserved, with reservations in farm leases, and exemption from all incidence of taxation; and so when present life forgets past life it is well to remind, and to draw attention to the ancient places that were chosen and entrenched by our forefathers.

Cranborne Chase is a peculiar district. It lies apart from railroads, and apart from most of the road traffic that passes through Ringwood or Salisbury. It is a solitary tract of down-land, corn-land, wood-land, and waste. Dry valleys run far up into the steep flanks of the chalk ridge that is the backbone of the Chase. Streams emerge with intermittent flow in the lower slopes of these valleys. With the exception of Ashmore, Shaftesbury, and Whitsbury, which are set on hilltops, the villages are scattered in the lowlands. Barrows, long and round: Camps of defence and of safety: Boundary banks and ditches: Pastoral enclosures: Cultivation banks: Roman roads: the sites of many British villages on the uplands, and Dykes of defence, all testify to the former habitation and desirability of this now solitary land. The evidence of its earthworks points to the assumption that a greater population was once settled on Cranborne Chase than is settled there now, and that it was under some sort of cultivation from prehistoric times.

We may gain an idea of the value possessed by this tract of country by considering its natural conditions.

On the East it was bounded by the New Forest. On the South by Holt Forest, and the heathland of Dorset. On the West by the Forest of Blackmore, and on the North by woodlands that probably covered the rich green-sand of the valley of the Nadder—Wastes and Forests that impeded the primitive cultivator, either from the poverty of their soil, or from the tangle of their growth. Amid such surroundings, the rolling chalk hills of Cranborne Chase must have emerged as a desirable land. The soil must have been the same then as now. A retentive loamy chalk ranging to a poor chalk, with clay-capped hills. The water supply must have been better than it is now. The rainfall we believe to have been greater, and the water-level we know, from the evidence of General Pitt-Rivers' excavations at Woodcuts, was higher then, than now. Think of the Tarrant, the Allen, the long Crichel, and the Gussage brooks, the Crane, the Martin Allen, the Rockbourne brook, the Ebble, the Donhead brook, the Iwerne brook, and the Pimperne brook. Think of all these streams flowing constantly fifty feet above their present rise, and you get a very different conception of the prehistoric pastoral and agricultural value of this tract of land. Looking back 2,000 years, we may imagine the area now known as Cranborne Chase as a fairly well watered downland, intersected by scattered woodland that stretched from Blagdon Hill to Holt, from Vernditch to Rushmore, and from Chettered to Ashmore. A truly desirable land when contrasted with its surroundings.

Such were the natural conditions of this tract of country which was chosen by the primitive herdsman and the subsequent cultivator, and the pastoral enclosures and cultivation banks are evidences of a tolerable security for settled possession. They imply that prehistoric men counted on folding their flocks and cattle on the same sites year in and year out, and on gaining the distant reward of laborious cultivation—on reaping where they had sown.

The Hill Camps, with their eminent positions, their great banks and deep ditches, and their concentration, appeal more to our imagination than do earthen folds and lynchets. But the latter were the outcome of the former. This land was desirable for pastoral and agricultural purposes; it was worth defending; and the ancient earthworks on Cranborne Chase proclaim the herdsman and the peaceful cultivator as much as the warrior.

The Roman occupation must have increased the habitable convenience of this district; for the Roman genius created communication with the outer world, and along the highways from Hamworthy and Dorchester came merchandise that furnished the demands of the Romano-British civilization. The excavations made by General Pitt-Rivers in the settlements of Woodcuts and of Woodyates, revealed accessories of life that suggest comfort, *e.g.*, timber and plaster houses, with roofs of shale or tile, hypocausts, furniture, metal-work, fine Samian pottery, glass, jewellery, oysters, etc. We may regard this district at the time of the Roman evacuation as having been thickly populated, peacefully occupied, and well cultivated, and we may attribute the stubborn resistance that later on was here offered to the oncoming West Saxon, as a testimony to the value of the territory which the Romanized Britons were defending.

THE ANCIENT EARTHWORKS OF CRANBORNE CHASE, 1–7

HAMBLEDON HILL

The natural approach to Hambledon Camp is on the South-Eastern side. Here the hill ridgeway forks into two spurs, one trending East towards Shroton, the other South-East towards the pass road leading from Steepleton to Hanford. Both these spurs are crossed from scarp to scarp by low banks and shallow ditches, double and triple, of which there are so many examples on Cranborne Chase.

The down outside the South-Eastern defences of Hambledon Hill Camp has been dinted with modern diggings for flints, and thus it is impossible to form an opinion as to what sort of habitation existed here to account for these outlying banks and ditches. But we may be fairly sure that these simple multiplications of low banks and shallow ditches belong to a different period to that of the great earthworks, so cunningly planned, that encircle and defend the approaches of the Camp on Hambledon Hill.

The South-Eastern defences of the Camp are very remarkable. For miles around the great inner bank is a landmark. It rises 30 feet above the bottom of the ditch, and 24 feet above the area, and beyond the double bank and ditch of this formidable earthwork there is a broad berm of 100 feet, very uneven in surface and protected at its South-Eastern extremity by two more great banks and ditches. The entrance passes through this outwork close to the Northern scarp of the ridge, and in such a way (see plan) that an enemy would be assailed for 200 yards on the flank by the defenders of the camp. The random digging of the berm between the inner camp lines and the outer defences is noticeable, and the sudden rise of the inner bank as it crosses the down ridge, with the rough scoops into the area—whence presumably came the earth—suggest emergency, and strengthening of existing defences. The Western entrance is also very strongly defended (see plan). In both cases these earthworks are in a fine state of preservation.

The Northern entrance of the Camp does not show signs of much usage. It must always have been inconvenient owing to its precipitous gradient. The South-Eastern and South-Western entrances were apparently the usual approaches, and on these the Camp defenders expended their utmost skill in fortification.

Within the Camp area—which at the Northern end rises nearly 100 feet above the triple entrenchments—there are some curious earthworks of debatable purpose, and a round barrow.

The long mound Northward of the said debatable earthworks is a doubtful long barrow. It may compare with the long mound within the area of Knap Hill Camp, excavated by Mr. and Mrs. Cunnington, and shown by the finds to have been thrown up at some time during or after the Roman period—probably as a shelter.

Shelter is a requirement that is forced on the attention of any modern excavator on these uplands. The wind sometimes sweeps and buffets across these bare downs with such rigour that it becomes almost unbearable; but as the digging proceeds, so shelter is obtained, both from the bank of upturned soil and from the excavated and lowered ground level. Thus protected, it is possible to dig in peace while the wind whistles through the bent grass above. Cattle need shelter as much as men; and it seems possible that the curious horseshoe form of bank, enclosing a sunken area, that may be found here, on Hambledon Hill, on Gussage Down, on Blandford Race-Down, on the Tarrant Hinton Downs, on Chettle Down, and at Buzbury Rings, may have been made for this elemental purpose.

It is impossible to write of Hod Hill and of Hambledon Hill and merely to expatiate on their prehistoric camps. Their names will always raise up visions of beauty, the memory of which abide as a possession to those who know these mighty earthworks. Hod Hill, with its bald, mound-like summit, here and there fringed with beech woods, dominating the Stour Valley, and rising abruptly, like a rampart above the still reaches of the winding river—Hambledon Hill, with its down scarps spotted with yews and thorn trees, with thickets of ash, elder, white beam, and yew, over which great wisps of Traveller's Joy fling their feathery tangle, with sheep feeding peacefully on the warlike camp, and hawks wivering in the pure air—while North, East, South, and West we gaze over hill, and vale, and down, and woodland that stretch and fade into far distance and vacant haze. So we praise these famous places, fortified by the toil and purpose of our forefathers in the ancient days when Time past unrecorded, except by such earthworks as we have been surveying, and by their makers' castaway possessions.

THE ANCIENT EARTHWORKS OF CRANBORNE CHASE, 15–17

CASTLE DITCHES (NEAR TISBURY)

Castle Ditches crown the summit of a steep greensand hill that projects from the base of Buxbury Hill. The site commands a long stretch of the Nadder Valley, and is about a mile and a half from Tisbury. Approached from this side, the camp defences are concealed by trees and underwood. A steep wooded hill, fringed along its flat top by wind-blown silver firs and larches, is all that can be seen. The woodland track that leads up to the area is abrupt, deeply sunken, and strongly defended. This approach seems to have been the water-way of the camp dwellers, for the springs rise at the bottom of the hill, where the greensand rests upon gault. On three sides the natural scarps of the hill have needed comparatively little work so as to shape them into a triple semicircle of defensive ramparts. But on the South-Eastern side the approach is flat, and across this plateau of easy access the entrenchments are multiplied. They are most perfect at the extreme Eastern side. Here, there are three great banks and ditches, reinforced by three outer banks and ditches of smaller size, protecting a winding entrance to the area—the whole of which is under cultivation. On the South-West side of this entrance there are now only four banks and ditches, cultivation apparently having destroyed the two outermost defences. Sir R. C. Hoare gives a plan of Castle Ditches in "Ancient Wiltshire," but it does not show this multiplication of entrenchments on the South-Eastern side. Presumably, as at Whitsbury, he was misled by the woodland growth—for these banks and ditches are concealed by underwood and by timber trees. When I made the section shown on the plan, the underwood had just been cut, which gave a fortunate opportunity for surveying this part of the camp.

All marks of habitation—if any existed—either within the area, or without, have been effaced by cultivation. A long mile of level upland connects Castle Ditches with Buxbury Hill—which is a projecting spur of the White Sheet Hill ridge, and the bank and ditch that cross Buxbury Hollow suggest defence against an enemy coming from these downs towards the camp.

Castle Ditches enclose one of the finest camps within the area of my survey. I think we may regard it as a British tribal centre, and pre-Roman. It is unfortunate in being concealed by woodlands, and in having such an indistinctive name. The place-name of Spelsbury (now forgotten), marked near the camp site in "Andrews and Dury's Map of Wiltshire," 1773, and in the similar map contained

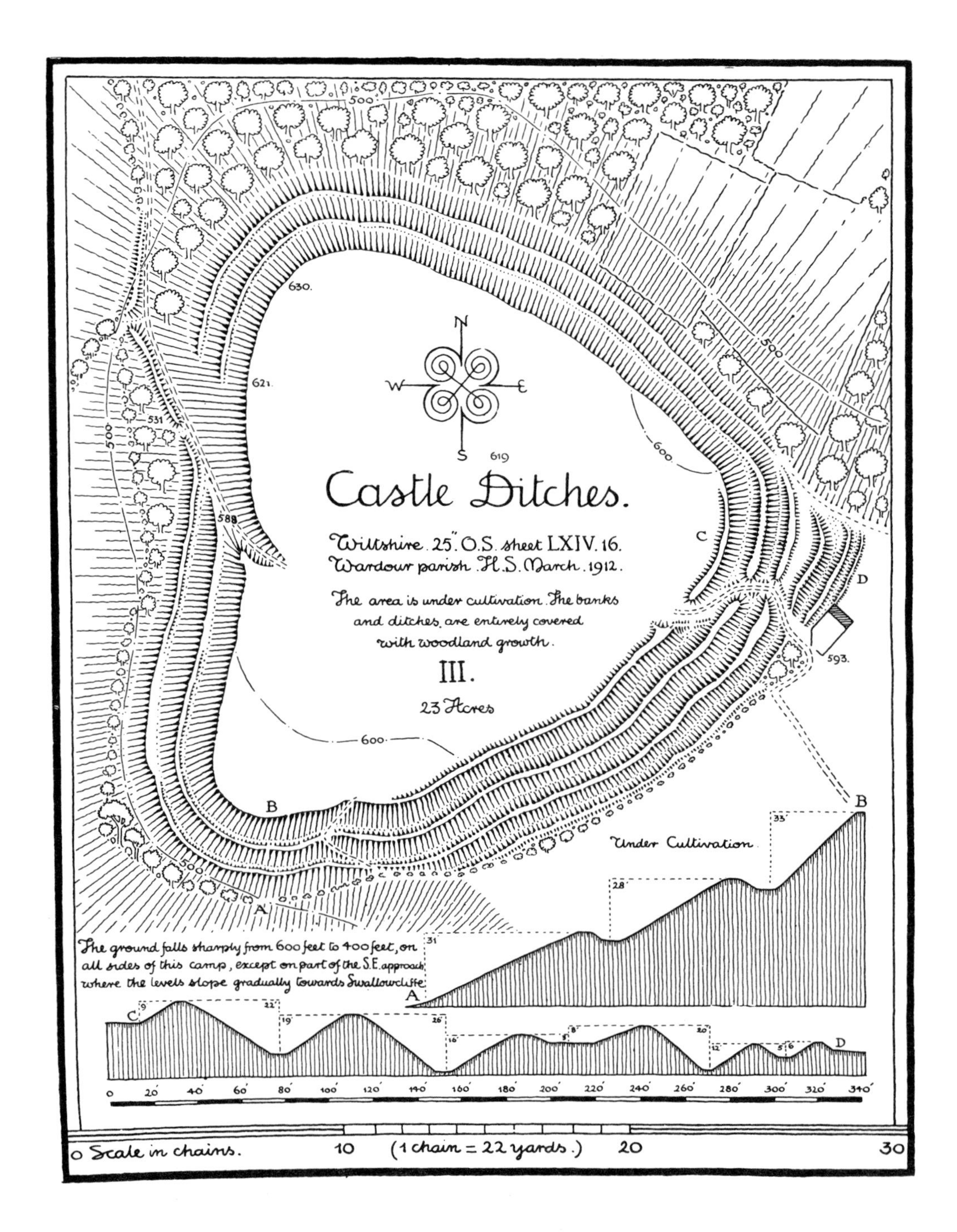
Castle Ditches.
Wiltshire. 25" O.S. sheet LXIV. 16.
Wardour parish. H.S. March. 1912.
The area is under cultivation. The banks and ditches are entirely covered with woodland growth.
III.
23 Acres
N
S
W
E
Under Cultivation
The ground falls sharply from 600 feet to 400 feet, on all sides of this camp, except on part of the S.E. approach where the levels slope gradually towards Swallowcliffe.
o Scale in chains.
10
(1 chain = 22 yards.)
20
30

in Gough's edition of "Camden's Britannia," 1789, suggests that this earthwork may formerly have been thus named. It may be noted that in neither of the maps mentioned above is this great camp marked, while both record the lesser camp of Chiselbury. A wood is shown in "Andrews and Dury's" map on the hill-top within the area of Castle Ditches, so probably the site was even more concealed then than now.

THE ANCIENT EARTHWORKS OF CRANBORNE CHASE, 17–18

BADBURY RINGS

Of the five principal camps within the district of my survey, namely, Hod, Hambledon, Castle Ditches (near Tisbury), Whitsbury Castle Ditches, and Badbury Rings, the last stands lowest above the sea; yet Badbury Rings are so isolated, and are situated in such a spacious tract of surrounding lowland, that their pine-crowned summit of 327 feet tells as a landmark for miles around—a distinction missed by Castle Ditches (near Tisbury), though the area of this camp rises to 630 feet—7 feet higher than Hambledon Hill.

Badbury Rings have been described in the *Dorset Field Club Proceedings*, vols. xi and xxvii, and in *Ancient Dorset*, by Charles Warne. So far as I know, their varied occupation has not been proved by excavation, but their origin has generally been accepted as pre-Roman. They are surrounded by a triple ring of great banks and deep ditches. There is a wide space between the outermost ring and the two inner rings. The Eastern entrance is a straightforward passage through the three lines of entrenchment. There are two entrances on the Western side. One, winding through the middle ring, that has a berm-like projection at this place; the other, leading straightforward through the Rings. This latter has been doubted as an original entrance, but it seems possible (in view of Mr. and Mrs. Cunnington's excavations on Knap Hill, near Devizes) that it may be original, and may have been used for driving cattle into the area at times of danger, and then these entrance gaps in the rings would have been stockaded.

This camp shows no signs of Roman adaptation, though the site was probably used, or occupied, by the Romans, for three of their roads converge here, namely, the main road from Sorbiodunum (Sarum) to Durnovaria (Dorchester), called Ackling Dyke, as it crosses the downs towards Woodyates; a road to Morionio (Hamworthy); and a branch road traceable across Abbeycroft Down, Hogstock, Launceston, Eastbury Park, Bussey Stool Park, Ashmore Common, and lost after Donhead Hollow, where it is last traceable, pointing towards Grovely Ridge. The wasted earthworks outside the Rings, on the Western side, do not seem to have any connection with the camp defences.

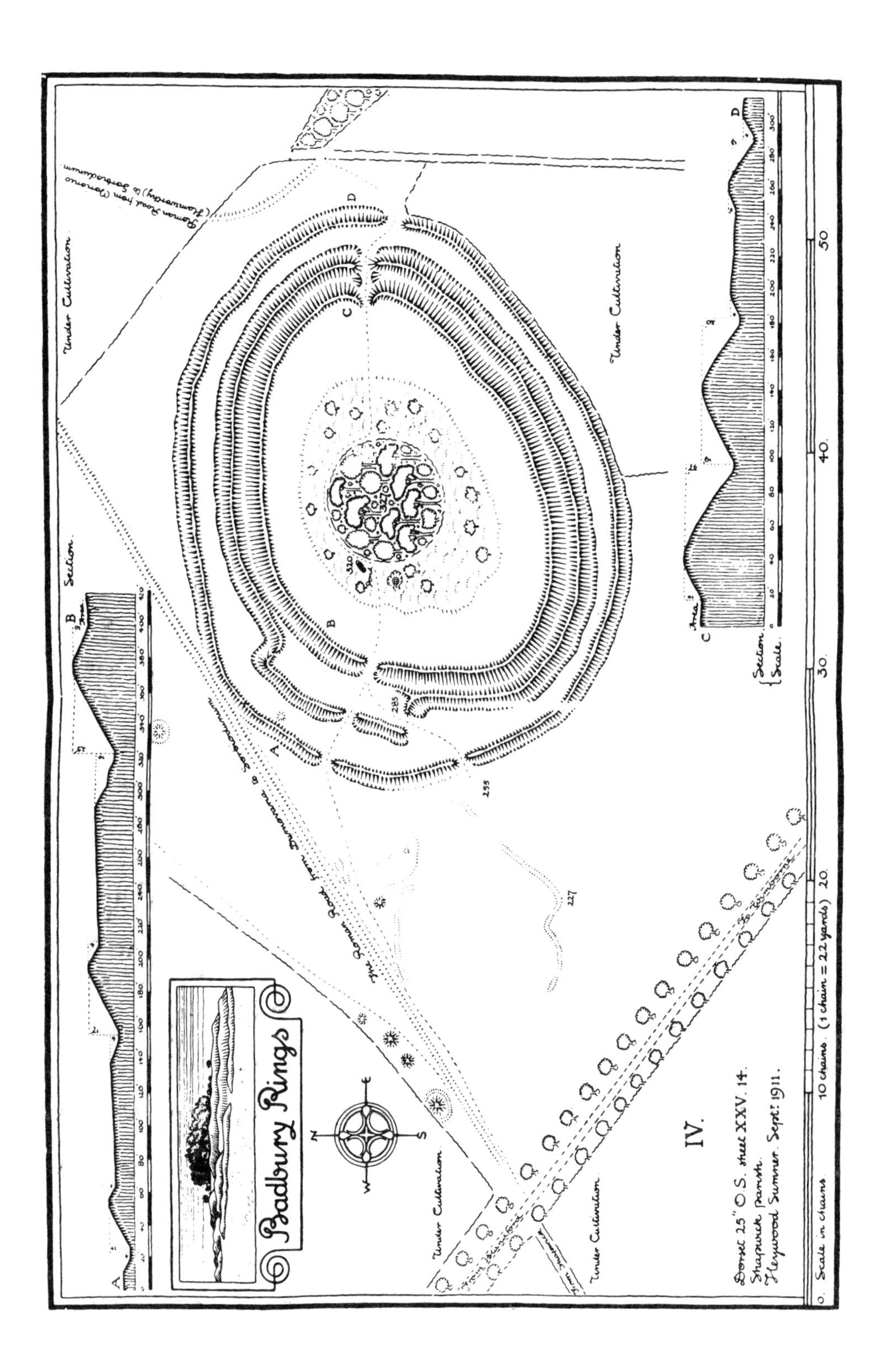
Badbury Rings
IV.
Under Cultivation
Under Cultivation
Under Cultivation
Under Cultivation
Section
Dorset 25" O.S. sheet XXV. 14.
Shapwick parish.
Heywood Sumner. Sept. 1911.
Section
Scale
Scale in chains
10 chains (1 chain = 22 yards)

Dr. Guest, in his essay on the "Early English Settlements in South Britain" (*Origines Celticae*, vol.ii), gives weighty reasons for his conjecture that Badbury was the site of the siege and battle of Mons Badonicus, A.D. 520, recorded by Gildas—a battle which stayed the onward western advance of the West Saxons for nearly half a century. Dr. Guest's reasoning is convincing to one who knows this country and the great fortresses and forests that lay between Charford on the Salisbury Avon, and Bath on the Bristol Avon (which latter site has been claimed as Mons Badonicus). It is difficult to imagine that within a year of the battle of Charford, A.D. 519, the West Saxons could have advanced sixty miles inland, across the strongly fortified downs of Cranborne Chase, through the dense forests of Blackmore Vale, past the Great Camp at Cadbury, and so on to Bath. A defeat, then, at Bath, must have meant annihilation to the invaders—whereas a defeat at Badbury would have merely meant a retreat to the Avon, twelve miles distant to the East, and to the New Forest borders, which presumably had at that time been conquered by the West Saxons, and where they were within easy access of the sea—and this is what actually appears to have happened.

THE ANCIENT EARTHWORKS OF CRANBORNE CHASE, 18–20

BUZBURY RINGS

Buzbury Rings are about two miles distant from Blandford, and the upland road, thence to Wimborne, passes through the outer part of the camp. The inner camp appears to have been the place of habitation, and here potsherds of various kinds may be picked up on the rabbit-scrapes and mole-hills. Many of these sherds seem to be of the early British type, handmade, imperfectly baked, and made of clay mixed with siliceous granules—suggesting an early occupation. The outer camp extends on the Northern and Eastern sides, and shows no signs of habitation, but was probably used for pastoral purposes. Buzbury Rings have been cut about by road-makers and by cultivators, but their general disposition is still fairly discernible. The camp shows no signs of having been strengthened, and its broad-topped low banks (six feet average height) and shallow ditches give us an idea of a British tribal camp that combined safety with pastoral requirements.

The site is pastoral rather than defensive, and if desperate emergency arose, it is intelligible that Badbury Rings (five miles to the South) or Hod Hill and Hambledon Hill (five miles to the North) would be chosen as camps of safety, or as camps to be strengthened rather than Buzbury. I do not think that this earthwork played much part in resisting the West Saxon advance westward in the sixth century.

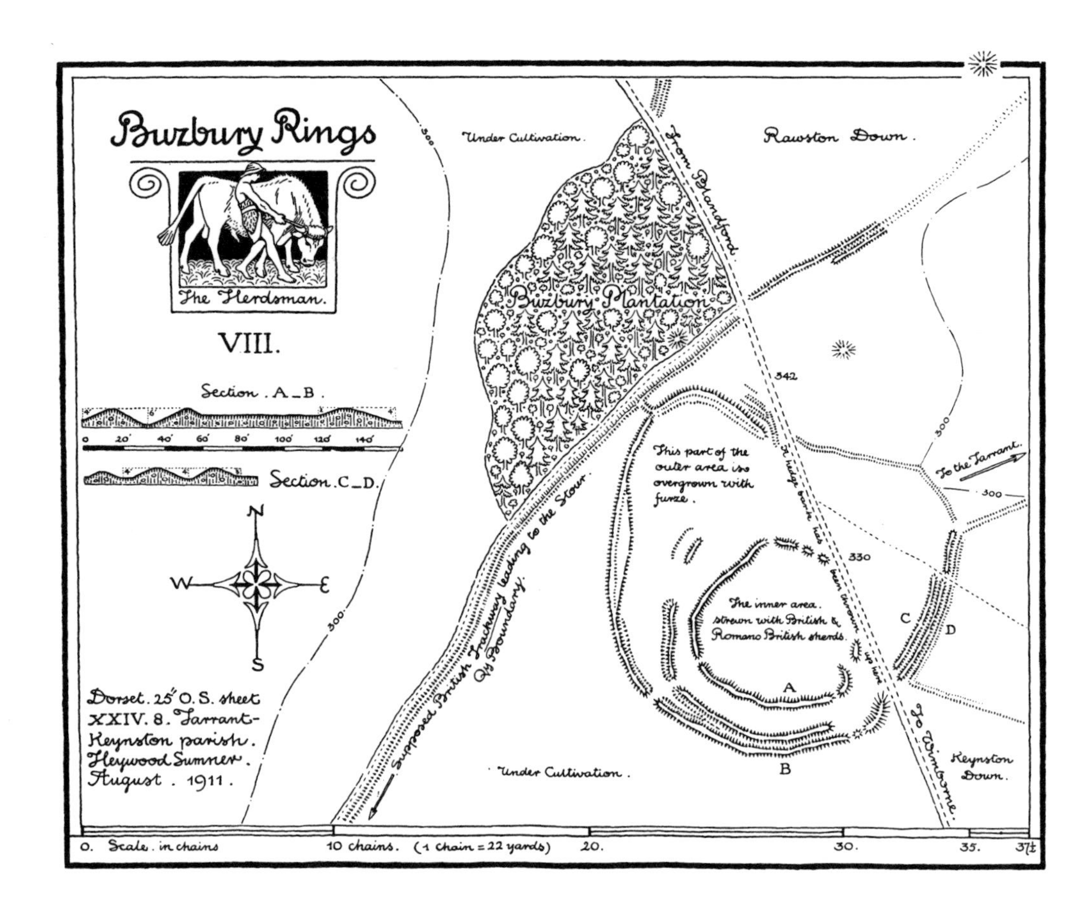

Banks and ditches of the Grim's Ditch type converge on Buzbury Rings. The Ordnance Survey marks one that approaches from Langton Long as "Supposed British Trackway." It continues on the North-Eastern side of the Blandford and Wimborne Road, pointing towards Blandford Race-down. Another appears to lead towards the Tarrant Valley, and another may be traced, under cultivation, towards Spettisbury Ring. The all-over surface measurements of these continuous banks and ditches compare with those through which I have cut sections on Knoll Down and on Gallows Hill. They would appear to be boundary divisions for pastoral purposes. Similar convergence of such earthworks towards centres of British habitation may be noted at Whitsbury Castle Ditches, and at the British settlements on Blandford Race-down, South Tarrant Hinton Down, Gussage Down, near Bokerly Dyke (South-West side), and Middle Chase Farm.

KNOWLTON

It is doubtful whether Knowlton was within the ancient outbounds of Cranborne Chase. The place-names of the perambulation are dubious here. Even the local knowledge of Dr. Wake Smart was baffled in their identification. But it is so near to the limits of our district that a few yards may be conceded, and we may take the benefit of the doubt.

For it is a benefit. It enables us to consider a most remarkable site—remarkable in this respect. Nowhere on Cranborne Chase, excepting, perhaps, the disk barrows near Woodyates, do we find any earthwork expression of what is supposed to be prehistoric formular religion. Circles, either marked by stones, or wrought in earth, are the signs of the unknown religion of our forefathers. Here, at Knowlton, surrounded by barrows, we have four circular earthworks, only one of which is still perfect, the others having been destroyed by cultivation. But from the remnant that remains, and from the situation, we cannot suppose that purposes of defence or of cattle enclosure were the motives of the makers of these rings. The two (apparently) original entrances of the one perfect remaining circle are opposite each other. The wide ditch is on the inside. The bank is unusually broad and precise in its circling enclosure. There is no similarity in its construction to that of any of the other earthworks on Cranborne Chase. Warne attributed these Rings at Knowlton to the Druids. But the Druids are so incapable of proof by means of excavation, that it is now usual to avoid them, and to take refuge in "some form of solar religion." The distinction may represent a difference. It is difficult to appreciate. It is possible, however, to appreciate the absolute difference in design between these earthworks and the others included in our survey. These that we are considering express a precision, apart from defensive or pastoral purposes, that embodies a new motive in construction, and the vague knowledge that we have of the Druids from Caesar, tells us that they introduced precise forms of religious observance and of government. And circles seem to have played a part in their formular expression. When we pass the wine with the Deisal turn, we perhaps unconsciously acknowledge Druidical belief. And so, also, when we look askant at the Tuaphol turn or Widdershins. There seems to be a different directing mind expressed in the making of these ringed earthworks, with their ditches on the inside, from that of the British camps and settlements and cattle enclosures.

In Hadrian Allcroft's *Earthwork of England*, there are two illuminating chapters on Miscellaneous Earthworks, in the second of which he discusses these Rings at Knowlton, and shows how they compare in certain particulars with those at

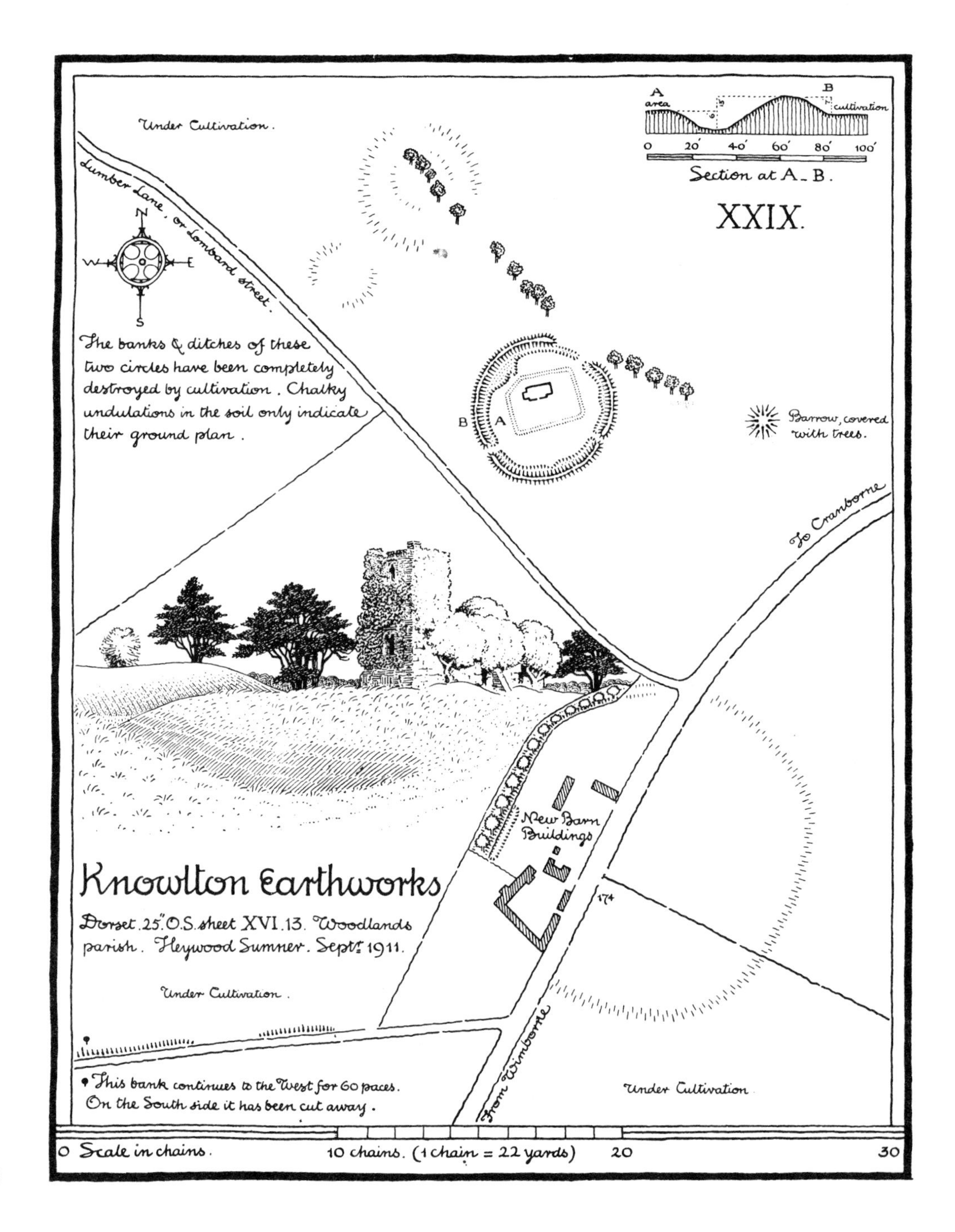
Under Cultivation.
Lumber Lane, or Lombard Street.
N
W
E
S
Section at A_B.
XXIX.
A
area
B
cultivation
0 20' 40' 60' 80' 100'
The banks & ditches of these two circles have been completely destroyed by cultivation. Chalky undulations in the soil only indicate their ground plan.
B
A
Barrow, covered with trees.
To Cranborne
New Barn Buildings
Knowlton Earthworks
Dorset. 25". O.S. sheet XVI.13. Woodlands parish. Heywood Sumner. Septr. 1911.
174
Under Cultivation.
From Wimborne
This bank continues to the West for 60 paces. On the South side it has been cut away.
Under Cultivation
0 Scale in chains. 10 chains. (1 chain = 22 yards) 20 30

Thornborough Moor, near Ripon, and with the camp at Figsbury Ring, near Salisbury. To this chapter I desire to refer my reader.

Two of the destroyed Rings at Knowlton are practically effaced. They are now merely circular undulations on arable land. But the largest of the four still suggests its original construction in one place—at the back of New Barn Buildings. Here, for a short space, both the outer bank and the inside ditch of this Ring are partially discernible.

Knowlton has given its name to a Hundred—showing that it was a place of special significance in Anglo-Saxon times. Subsequently, probably in the fourteenth century, a little stone church was built within the area of the circle that still remains, and it is further surrounded by a low, oblong bank. Particulars of its ecclesiastical vicissitudes may be found in Hutchins's *History of Dorset*, vol. iii. The site of this ruined Christian church, standing within an earthen circle that seems to belong to the unknown religion of the early Britons, and guarded without by a row of ancient yew trees, is indeed most beautiful, and it marks the strange changes and chances that have happened during the lapse of 2,000 years.

Reference to the plan of Knowlton will show that these circles are surrounded by barrows—like Stonehenge and like Avebury. But it must also be noted that this site does not now appear as the barrow centre of Cranborne Chase—as Stonehenge is the barrow centre of Salisbury Plain. That distinction belongs to Oakley Down below Pentridge, near Worbarrow.

THE ANCIENT EARTHWORKS OF CRANBORNE CHASE, 46–7

THE MIZMAZE ON BREAMORE DOWN

In Hereford Cathedral there is a thirteenth-century map of the world on which, amongst many strange geographical shapes, is figured the island of Crete, with a labyrinth plan, and the inscription "Laborintus id est domus Dealli." The Breamore Mizmaze is similar to this Hereford labyrinth plan, and also to the following grass-cut mazes in England, namely, at Alkborough, Lincolnshire, at Broughton Green, Northants, at Ripon Common (now destroyed), and to the pavement mazes in French churches at S. Quentin and at Chartres, and to one that is incised on the Cathedral of Lucca.

The device of a labyrinth first appears in the fifth or sixth century B.C. on Cretan coins; and the earliest that we read of was "The Cretan Labyrinth built by Daedalus, in imitation of a more ancient Labyrinth in Egypt, by command of King Minos. First, it served as a prison for the monster Minotaur, then as an architectural web to enclose Daedalus, whence he was enabled to escape by aid of

The Mizmaze on Breamore Down XXXII.

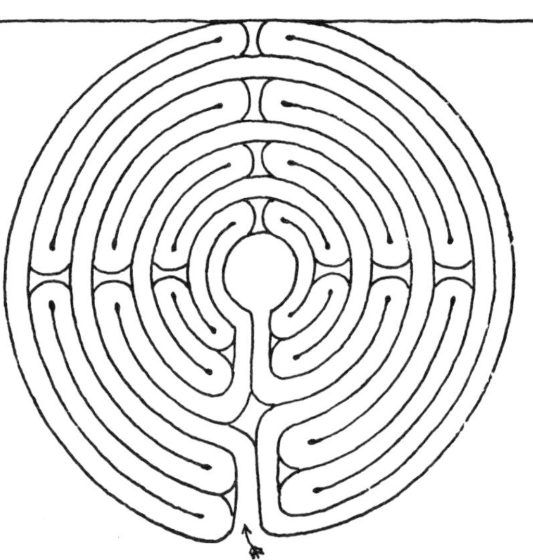

artificial wings" (Trollope, *Journal of Archaeology*, vol. xv, from whom my further quotations also are taken). Herodotus describes an Egyptian architectural labyrinth at Lake Maeris. Pliny alludes to an architectural labyrinth for royal sepulchres both in the island of Lemnos and of Samos. Thus the early uses of labyrinths seem to have been as prisons and as burial-places.

The labyrinth at Lucca, already referred to, marks a new departure in the signification of the design. It is incised on the porch pier of the Cathedral. The centre is filled by Theseus and the Minotaur (nearly effaced), and at the side is the following inscription:

> Hic quem Creticus edit Dedalus est Laberintus,
> De quo nullus vadere quivit qui fuit intus,
> Ni Theseus gratis Ariane stamine Jutus.

The Church now further appropriated the Pagan labyrinth, and instead of the Minotaur, "Sancta Ecclesia," or the Cross, was inscribed as the centre of the design, which was "deemed to be indicative of the complicated folds of sin by which man is surrounded, and how impossible it would be to extricate himself from them except through the assisting hand of Providence."

Labyrinths were then frequently laid down in coloured marbles on church floors, *e.g.*, at S. Maria Trastevere, Rome, at Ravenna, at S. Quentin, at Chartres, at Rheims (1240, destroyed 1794), at Amiens (1288, destroyed 1825), etc.

Later on these labyrinths were used as instruments of penance for non-fulfilment of vows of pilgrimage to the Holy Land, and were called "Chemins de Jérusalem." The pilgrims followed the windings of the Maze on their knees, and the centre was called "Le Ciel." Some of these labyrinths were destroyed because "children by noisily tracking out their tortuous paths, occasioned disturbance during divine service."

We have no ancient example of an ecclesiastical labyrinth in any English church, but our turf-cut mazes are undoubtedly of mediaeval ecclesiastical origin. They are situated near a church or a monastic settlement, and still remain at Breamore, Alkborough, Wing, Boughton Green, Saffron Walden, Sneinton, and St. Catherine's Hill, Chilcombe, etc.

The priory of St Michael's, Breamore, was founded for Austin Canons about 1129, and the Mizmaze may be connected with the priory.

In Elizabethan times these English mazes would seem to have been secularized. Titania thus bears witness:

> The nine-men's-morris is filled up with mud;
> And the quaint mazes in the wanton green,
> For lack of tread, are undistinguishable.

The local name for them was "Julian Bower," "Troy Town" (Troi in Welsh means "to turn"), "Shepherd's Race," or "Mizmaze." The Renaissance garden mazes, in which the paths were misleading, have no relation to the labyrinth type, in which the paths always lead continuously to the centre of the design.

THE ANCIENT EARTHWORKS OF CRANBORNE CHASE, 52–3

EARTHWORKS OF THE NEW FOREST

"'Tis distance lends enchantment to the view." The far limits of a landscape fade into undefined regions of romance. We gaze, and we name supposed landmarks. We guess at forms that rise and fall along the horizon. Are they hills? Are they clouds? What lies beyond them? The possibility of some unknown wonder always seems to haunt the blue distance.

In somewhat similar manner do romance and wonder haunt the distant past. Beyond the written records of man stretch vast periods of silence—yet not wholly unbroken. Writings cease; but stone, earth, pottery and metal still testify man's handiwork, and proclaim the far horizon. The crude wonder that has ascribed the origin of these silent witnesses to the Devil, to Giants, and to Fairies, suggests the spell of mystery and enchantment that veils the outline of prehistoric times. We also wonder—but with a difference. The romance of knowledge pursued is greater than that of credulity, and observant curiosity is the first step on the road to knowledge. To us the unrecorded Past is haunted by questions. What manner of men were our forefathers? By whom and for what purpose was this or that earthwork made? How did their makers live? The answers to such questions must be found in our right understanding of their derelict handicraft and of their earthworks; in our right comparison of the evidence found in different districts; in our right deductions as we pass from the known into the unknown; and if we have such observant curiosity we shall find that the evidence of derelict handicraft, *i.e.* of flints showing sure signs of human work in fashioning, hacking and chipping, reaches immeasurably farther into the mists that shroud the Past than does the evidence of earthworks.

If ghosts revisit the scenes of their earthly sojourn, the makers of ancient earthworks must wonder at the oblivion into which their labours have fallen. They are forgotten. They abide by chance. They are used at will. Here, a rampart provides holiday-makers with a grassy slither, and boys and girls shoot down the scarp, and then re-scale the rampart in order to repeat the descent. There, a cart-track crosses an earthwork, and wheel-ruts and trampling have reduced its profile to mere undulation. Here, random spade-work proclaims ferretting, or the digging out of a hunted fox. There, tons of chalk have been taken for the land. Elsewhere the persistent plough or the planter's spade have been at work along obstructing banks and ditches, until the rough places have been made smooth. Holiday-maker, wayfarer, keeper, farmer, and forester, all intent on their respective purposes, and all oblivious to their careless damage as they mis-use landmarks which bear witness to the valour, the reverence, and the forethought of our ancestors.

Still, from time to time the ghosts would be cheered. They would welcome perplexed archaeologists, puzzling over their earthworks, measuring them, and devoting full attention to their handiwork. But their welcome might be confounded when some formerly perplexed archaeologist returned to the site, now confidently expounding his theories to a Field Club congregation!

They would welcome also the Ordnance Surveyors accurately plotting their casual alignments, but the ghosts might smile perhaps, as they peeped, and saw *Roman camp* inscribed on the survey sheet.

Ancient earthworks are generally supposed to denote warfare. The purpose of the great earthen ramparts of the hill-tops has been attributed to the lesser landmarks of the plains. The clash of arms has been guessed beside boundary earthworks, habitation settlements, cattle enclosures, and barrows. Indeed our archaeological forefathers located traditional victories and defeats by existing groups and lines of barrows, thus imputing war where peace is really suggested, for elaborate obsequies in honour of the dead belong to periods of leisure. Certainly the earthwork evidence of warfare is more eminent and intelligible than that of peaceful pursuit; nevertheless the latter is wide spread, and careful investigation is gradually discovering the different purposes served in times past by banks, ditches, scarps, mounds, and hollows. We are learning to understand them as records of peace, as well as of war; and, as such, to recognize their value, although in size they may appear to be insignificant.

Elderly people of blameless life may be found who confess that they prefer Detective stories to Love stories. To such Field Archaeology should appeal. The zest of detection impels the attempt to understand ancient earthworks. They hold their secrets. We have to survey, to compare, and to excavate in order to discover their purpose. We have no written word to help us. Observation, comparison, and earth-delving are our only means of information; and the detective instinct is needed to divine their evidence. Tentative conclusions are possible, but certainty is not possible. Uncertainty, however, need not deter, for we may attain reasonable presumptions if we are observant, if we know where to look, if we know what to look for, if we are persistent, if we are discriminating, and if we are not hasty. Enthusiasm is the first thing needful for one who follows the somewhat solitary pursuit of Field Archaeology, but it must be trained, and it must eschew dogmatism. Solitary enthusiasm and pursuit tend to beget dogmatic opinion, and theories thus evolved to become crystallized, until the final stage of fixity is reached—when opinions are enforced as facts. A suspense account is necessary in archaeological matters. Opinions that we may form of wasted earthworks must be tentative; to be confirmed or contradicted by fuller knowledge; but if short cuts to conclusions are attempted, through guess with probability to assertion without proof, we shall probably be confounded by the evidence of some future excavation.

Now these general remarks apply to the survey of ancient earthworks here attempted. Peaceful purposes will be found in the following plans quite as often as war-like purposes, and our estimate of their significance will fail if we do not appreciate such different intentions, or if we only attach importance to size. Our estimates moreover must be more tentative than usual, for they can rarely be verified or corrected by excavation, because New Forest sites are so much overgrown with trees. Indeed, this superficial survey will be tantalizing—for we shall constantly be desiring to excavate without any possibility of performance.

But fuller knowledge of the Past can only be obtained by seeking in the right places; and a corrected survey of these sites is the first thing needful. Excavation is only rarely achieved, when good fortune favours the event. Meantime, the planning of an earthwork gives it a renewed chance of survival—of preservation. Attention is drawn to its existence and, at least, assurance is given that it has been held worthy of careful investigation in order to present and to preserve its record. Although our estimates of purpose and period may be uncertain, our record of survey should be approximately sure, and it includes several ancient earthworks which have not been planned, and which add to our knowledge of the prehistoric occupation of this district.

The earthworks of the New Forest district are neither eminent nor effective, like the earthen landmarks of the Downs. They are wasted by the elements, owing to the nature of the soil, and concealed by vegetation owing to the Forest. Even when they are set on high ground they are hidden by trees. With the exception of the barrows—or butts—which are conspicuous on the plains, they must be searched for, and, when found, they may be considered to be unimportant.

Still, though these earthworks may justly be described as of minor importance in regard to their size, and to their state of preservation, they have certain characteristics which deserve more attention than has hitherto been bestowed on them. They have variety; they have local character; and, moreover, they stand on barren land which has always defied cultivation; they have been undisturbed—except by tree-planting.

Such a setting would seem as though it must be an ideal hunting ground for the Field Archaeologist. But it is not. The soil is in fault; it is mainly Tertiary, and this formation of sand, gravel, and clay is always wasting beneath the elements. The heath, and furze, and sedge-grass, and bracken which cover the ground do not prevent waste—as the close mat of thistly grass prevents surface waste on the chalk downs. When heavy rain falls, the absorbing capacity of this soil is soon exhausted; the water begins to lie; then to flow; every rut becomes a runnel; every trackway becomes a watercourse; thus the surface waste of this sandy, peaty, clayey soil is unceasing, and thus the rough places tend to be made smooth, and the hillsides to be washed gradually downwards. Ancient earthworks are always wasting on the Tertiary formation, and their survey will be made with difficulty and discontent. Moreover the obstacles to survey are further multiplied in the New Forest by the recently planted inclosures which conceal these sites. The planter's spade has taken no heed of the "humpy" ground; while drain ditches, old trackways, saw-pits, stag parks, bee-gardens, and random gravel-diggings have also complicated the surface landmarks, or have cut about the evidence of ancient earthwork. Yet, notwithstanding all these drawbacks, we have one piece of rare good fortune here, for although the natural processes of waste are active, and although the lesser earthworks are almost covered by the fallen leaf-mould of years past, we have the advantage, as before said, of being able to examine a great expanse of wild country which has never been under cultivation.

THE ANCIENT EARTHWORKS OF THE NEW FOREST, 1–4

BUCKLAND RINGS

In referring to the plan of Buckland Rings it should be noted that the entrenchments are wholly concealed by timber trees, except on part of the eastern side where they have been levelled. Gilpin's phrase, "it gives no value to the scene" is still true. This fine camp is not a distant landmark, but it is well preserved in spite of its gravelly soil, and for this we have to thank the concealing trees. The middle rampart is unusually broad and would have afforded ample space for many defenders of this camp. Stone throwing from carefully prepared ramparts of vantage, and obstacles in the way of raiders, were the purposes of prehistoric entrenchments; concealment, and shelter from far-shot missiles are latter-day purposes. The omission of the third rampart and ditch on the western side appears to have been caused by the making of the road which skirts the camp here. We may assume that Buckland Rings belong to the comparatively rare class of camps encircled by triple entrenchments. The principal entrance was undoubtedly on the eastern side, with easy access to the probable dock at Passford Farm, 250 yards distant. There are four other gap entrances to the camps, all of which are shown in Gough's plan. None of them seem to be original. They suggest modern requirement, as certainly they fulfil it, but this could only be verified or disproved by excavation. The area contained by these entrenchments is about seven acres. Buckland Rings cannot claim to be the largest defensive camp in the New Forest district; Frankenbury has this distinction; but its premier claim is sure notwithstanding, in respect of its well-preserved triple entrenchments, and of its remarkable position in connection with Ampress. It is the finest defensive camp which will be delineated in the following survey.

The two-sided camp at Ampress has been overlooked by the Ordnance Survey, but is recorded by Dr. Williams-Freeman. Its single rampart has been much spread by cultivation, and the width of the spread suggests that it must originally have been a big bank. The ditch on the western side is well preserved, and unusually wide, while on the southern side it appears as the road-bed for the lane which leads to Ampress Waterworks. There is no entrance landwards now apparent, and none is shown in Gough's plan. On the northern and eastern sides of the area there are no signs of any entrenchment, but it ends with an abrupt scarp that descends about ten feet to swampy ground through which flow the Lymington River and Passford brook. This scarp is due to the scour of ancient tides which flowed inland more freely formerly than nowadays.

The waterworks above mentioned are situated at the north-eastern corner of the Camp area. It was very disappointing to find, after many enquiries, that the only relic found in digging the foundations, was a William and Mary coin. Yet this interesting camp must hold its secrets underground. Excavation for knowledge on this site may some day lead to the discovery of its unknown origin and occupation. Indeed both Ampress and Buckland Rings could be excavated—which cannot be said of most New Forest sites. The ramparts at the entrance of Buckland Rings have been ploughed and spread, but they are not overgrown by trees, and beneath these wasted entrenchments the ditches would be revealed intact, and evidence in the shape of castaway relics would presumably be found that would give us knowledge of its past where now we have none. The example of Mr. and Mrs. B. H. Cunnington in Wiltshire needs followers in Hampshire.

Meantime, pending the chance of future excavation, it may be permissible to

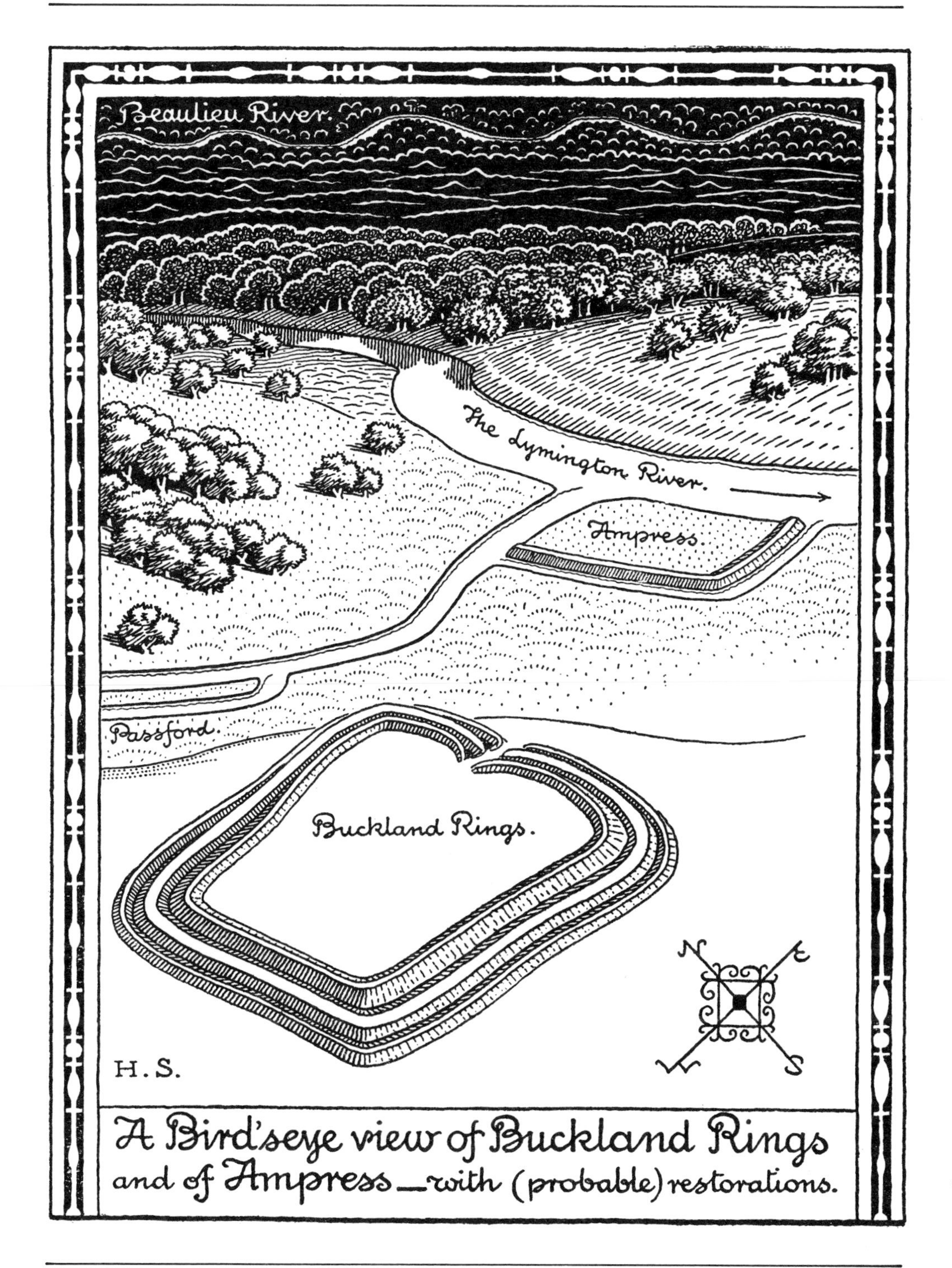

A Bird'seye view of Buckland Rings and of Ampress – with (probable) restorations.

speculate. Enemies may be entrenched in close proximity one against the other, as we know by bitter experience. Ampress appears to be a sea-faring invaders' camp. The apparent absence of any entrance on the landward sides; the big rampart and the wide ditch, which would have been a wet moat when the Lymington River was estuarine; the undefended area on the seaward sides; all these features indicate usage by sea-faring invaders. In *Earthwork of England*, p. 379, Mr. Hadrian Allcroft says: "There is no single form of earthwork which can be said to be more suggestive of the Saxon than of other peoples, earlier or later, unless it be the wet moat." It seems possible that the Saxon, or Jutish invaders, whom we know cruised along these southern shores in the fourth, fifth, and sixth centuries A.D., may have sailed up the Lymington estuary, blockaded the Britons' ships in Passford dock, and entrenched themselves at Ampress protected by a rampart and wet moat. Their subsequent inland advance, and area of settlement on the mainland may be indicated by the large number of *ton* place-names which exist along the coast from Lymington to Christchurch.

Buckland Rings, on the other hand, appear to be pre-Roman, and the rectangular form of the camp, that is made much of in Richard Warner's assumptions, may be attributed to the natural, ground-plan shape of the bluff on which it stands. The ancient pasturage for cattle would presumably have been on the low-lying grounds along the Lymington River and the sea-coast, and the principal entrance was on this side. Passford dock may have been used for the shipping of the Britons who occupied this camp.

The Bird's-eye view of Buckland Rings and Ampress given here is an attempt to reconstruct the essential features of these Entrenchments, set in their primitive surroundings.

THE ANCIENT EARTHWORKS OF THE NEW FOREST, 17–19

CASTLE PIECE, ROE WOOD

This camp is situated on a gentle slope above the little stream that rises in Milkham Inclosure, flows through Roe Wood and Greenford bottom, and eventually becomes the Linford Brook, joining the Avon above Ringwood. It stands about 200 feet above the sea, on a site that does not especially suggest defence. The ground rises gradually to the east, from 200 feet at Castle Piece to 300 feet on Bratley Plain, about a mile distant. The entrenchments are much spread owing to the wasting nature of the soil, which is a sandy, gravelly clay; but they are plainly defined all round the camp, and the entrance with its incurving bank is unmistakable. The over-all measurement of the rampart and ditch is

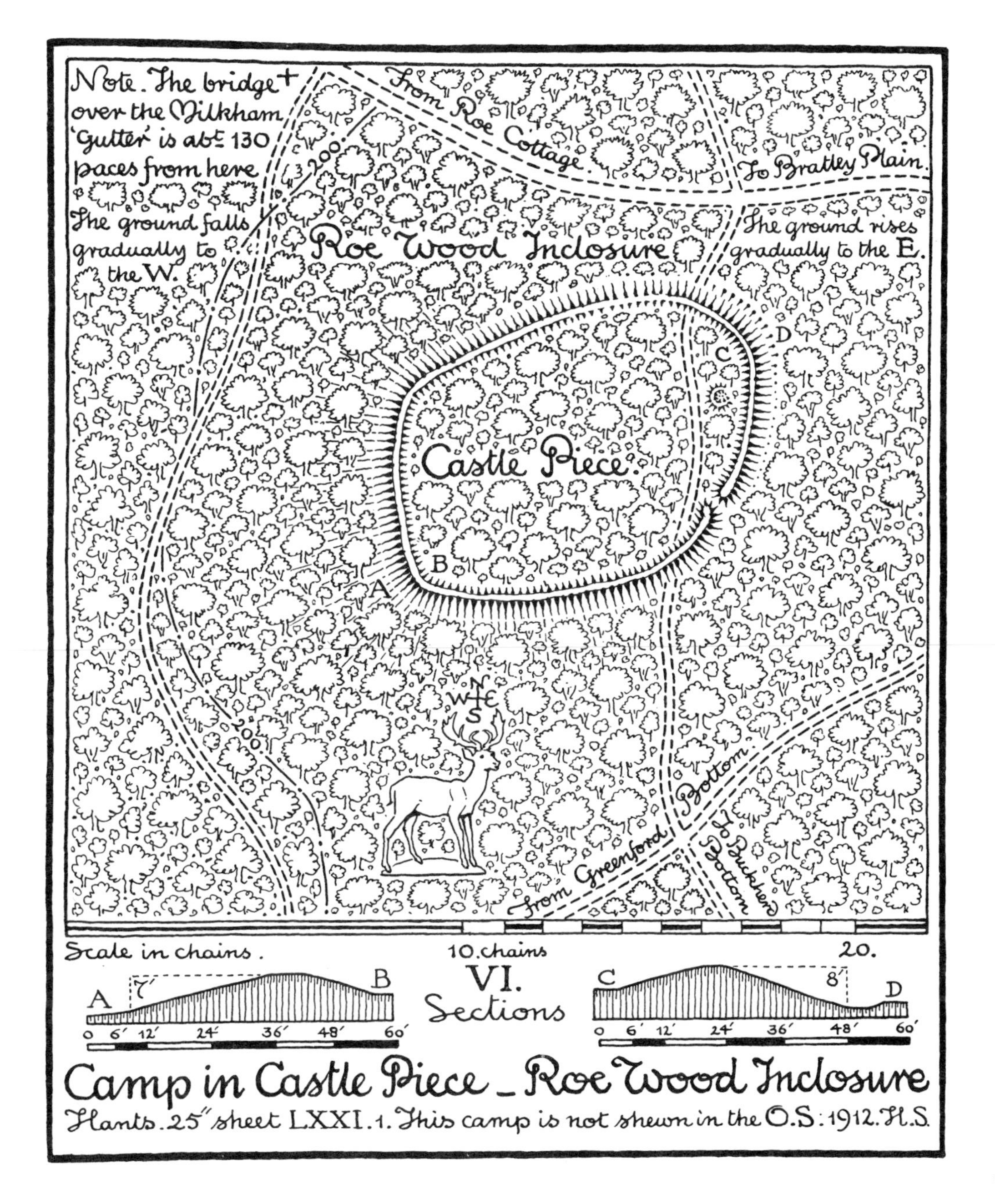
Note. The bridge + over the Milkham 'Gutter' is abt. 130 paces from here
The ground falls gradually to the W.
From Roe Cottage
To Bratley Plain
The ground rises gradually to the E.
Roe Wood Inclosure
Castle Piece
A
B
C
D
200
N
W
E
S
Bottom
From Greenford
Buckherd Bottom
Scale in chains.
10. chains
20.
VI.
Sections
7'
8'
0 6' 12' 24' 36' 48' 60'
Camp in Castle Piece _ Roe Wood Inclosure
Hants. 25" sheet LXXI. 1. This camp is not shewn in the O.S: 1912. H.S.

considerable, and testifies to a big entrenchment when they were originally constructed. The whole site has been planted, and is now overgrown with oak, Scots pine, and thorn-bushes. The area contains about 4½ acres. In summer it is concealed beneath bracken, but in winter or spring the entrenchments can be traced, though the woodland tangle of thorn-bushes opposes a prickly barrier to an exact survey. On the eastern side of the area, close to the ride, there is a circular banked depression, seven paces in diameter, that suggests a hut-pit dwelling. The barrows on Bratley Plain, and on Rockford Common, one mile, and two miles distant respectively, denote Bronze Age occupation in this district, to which period this camp may belong.

Castle Piece seems to compare with the camp in Mistleberry Wood, near Handley, on Cranborne Chase, about fourteen miles distant to the west—though the entrenchments of Mistleberry are much better preserved. But the over-all measurements of their respective rampart and ditch coincide; the areas are approximate in size—Castle Piece being the larger; in both instances the shape of these camps is not determined by the rise and fall of the ground. Both of them are circular, because probably, this shape was traditional. These camps appear to belong to the type which Dr. Williams-Freeman classifies as Woodland Ring Works, and may be assumed to be pre-Roman and defensive.

THE ANCIENT EARTHWORKS OF THE NEW FOREST, 26

SLODEN HILL-SIDE ENCLOSURE

Sloden, Crock Hill, Islands Thorns, and Ashley Rails, Pitts Wood, are the principal sites where the New Forest Potters plied their craft during the early centuries of our era. These sites may be found in the northern corner of the Forest, about five miles east of Fordingbridge, and six miles south-east of Downton. The district belongs geologically to the Tertiary formation, with occasional hill-top capping of Quaternary drift gravel. The soil varies from Barton clay at Sloden and Amberwood to Bagshot sands at Pitts Wood, and from Bracklesham Beds at Crock Hill and Islands Thorns to plateau gravel (Quaternary drift) at Ashley Cross. The kiln sites at Sloden and at Islands Thorns are on hillsides, about 300 feet above the sea, and at Crock Hill and at Pitts Wood beside constant streams, about 220 feet above the sea. The present distribution of woodland and heathland probably indicates the prehistoric distribution of growth, for the modern Forest Inclosures occupy the best soil in this district, *i.e.*, soil that would always have grown timber, while the sandy heathland would have only grown thickets.

Along the top of Sloden Hill there stands an old wood of great beauty and variety, which may be the remains of tree-planting done in the reign of Henry VIII, or of Queen Elizabeth. Sloden Inclosure was planted in 1864, Crock Hill and Islands Thorns in 1852, Amberwood in 1815, and Pitts Wood in 1775. The 6-inch Ordnance Survey sheet marks, "supposed site of the ancient town of Sloden," in the centre of the Inclosure, "church-yard" near the eastern corner of the Inclosure, and "Roman pottery found" at the western verge of Crock Hill Inclosure. Besides these inscriptions, it gives no indications of the various pottery sites, nor of any earthworks at Sloden.

In *Archaeologia*, vol. xxxv, there is a map that illustrates a paper by Rev. J. Pemberton Bartlett, "Excavations on the site of some Ancient Potteries," which supplies useful information, but does not show any earthworks at Sloden. In *The New Forest*, by J. R. Wise, there is a slight plan of intersecting banks on Sloden Hillside, and his general description suggests that there was much more to be seen when he wrote *circa* 1860—before the Inclosure was made—than is to be seen now.

Such being the mapped record of the New Forest Pottery sites it seemed desirable to trace and to distinguish the wasted and cut-about banks that may still be found at Sloden. British camps, barrows, and defensive dykes may appear to be of major importance, while wasted earthworks, such as these, may hardly seem even to be of minor importance, but all earthworks, if rightly understood, record ways of life, and we want to understand how our forefathers lived, as well as how they fought, and were commemorated. This is the province of the Field Archaeologist. He must trace and decipher the blurred earthen records that lie forgotten on our land, whether of "major" or of "minor" importance, and he must know his country both above ground and below—for habitation and livelihood have always been governed by soil, and rock, and water. The ardour and uncertainty of the Chase belong to this search for the past, and the zest of detection to this reading of earth; and the farther afield that the seeker knows his district, the better able will he be to interpret, comparatively, the local significance of its ancient earthworks.

Two large embanked areas may still be traced near the Sloden pottery sites, and they need to be carefully distinguished. The smaller of the two actually encloses these sites within its area of about 60 acres on the top of Sloden Hill. The other lies just outside the pottery sites on the northern slopes of Sloden and of Whiteshoot Hills, and encloses about 350 acres. For the sake of distinction these are here designated respectively, *Sloden hill-top Inclosure*, and *Sloden hill-side Enclosure*.

The earthworks of *Sloden hill-top Inclosure* are much wasted. They consist of a small, consolidated bank with a ditch on the outside of the area enclosed, and with an over-all measurement of 15 to 16 feet, which is the same measurement as that of a modern Forest Inclosure bank and ditch. The bank rises about 2 feet above the silted-up bottom of the ditch. The scale of this earthwork is similar throughout its course which can be traced continuously. Its alignment is fairly regular, and the corners are wide and rounded. This inclosure contains about 60 acres; it was probably made in the reign of Henry VIII or of Queen Elizabeth, and compares in every respect with the wasted earthwork that may be traced round the outskirts of Ridley Wood. In *A brief History of the Arboriculture of the New Forest, Hampshire*, by the Hon. Gerald Lascelles, late Deputy Surveyor, will be found interesting extracts from presentments referring to these old encoppicements, or inclosures. An observant perambulation of Sloden or of Ridley Wood will afford proof that Mr. Lascelles is right in his contention that we owe the present beauty of these old woods to this practice of encoppicements, or inclosures for tree-planting—a practice which may have begun as early as A.D. 1437.

The earthworks of *Sloden hill-side Enclosure* are different to the above both in construction and in alignment. They consist of a broad, consolidated bank with a ditch on the outside of the area enclosed, in places with a slight bank on the counterscarp, and with an over-all measurement of about 30 feet. The bank rises about 3 feet above the silted-up bottom of the ditch. The alignment is irregular. At Whiteshoot Bottom (near Eyeworth powder works), the usual bank and ditch construction of this earthwork changes, and runs for 300 paces in a straight line across boggy ground, as a broad, consolidated, low bank, 14 feet across, with slight ditches on either side, and an over-all measurement of about 26 feet. Reference to Plan VIII will show that at both the eastern and western extremities of this enclosure its bank and ditch terminate at the Latchmore Brook. Three embanked sides can be traced continuously, while there are no signs of embankment on the fourth side. Probably when this large enclosure was originally made, a swamp marked the line of the brook. The present-day channel of the Latchmore Brook is artificially cut throughout these inclosures, which suggests the swampy nature of this valley in recent times, and probably it was a bog 1,800 years ago. Perhaps felled trees were used as a boundary along the swamp side of the enclosure. If this explanation is accepted, and if the brook is taken as the boundary limit on the northern side, the area of Sloden hill-side enclosure amounts to about 350 acres. It appears to have been made for pastoral purposes, and to belong to the period when the pottery sites were occupied by the Romano-British. The entrance to this vast enclosure is nowhere clearly defined. This uncertainty is owing to the wide rides, and to the attendant tree-planting of Sloden inclosure, but I am inclined to place it at the eastern intersection of the

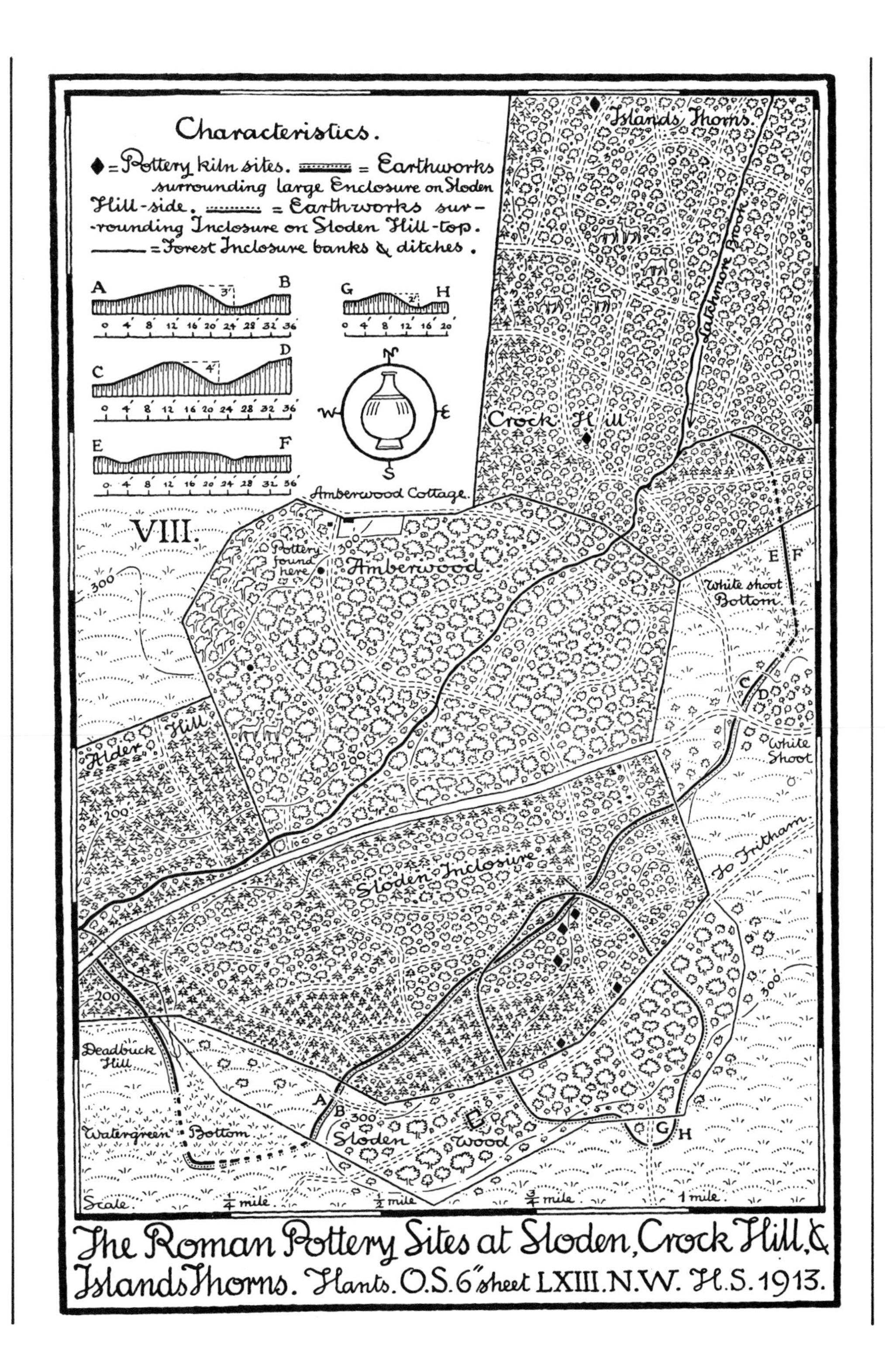

The Roman Pottery Sites at Sloden, Crock Hill, & Islands Thorns. Hants. O.S. 6" sheet LXIII. N.W. H.S. 1913.

enclosure with the *inclosure*. Here is a return bank that may compare with the return cattle-stop bank on Gorley Hill. At the latter site the return bank is outside the enclosure bank, and is intelligible as a wing cattle-stop—to and from the drinking place. This is inside the vast enclosure (which included drinking access for 1½ miles). However, exigencies of cattle-driving which we cannot now appreciate may have dictated such planning. Whatever the purpose, this feature is noteworthy, occurring (reversed) in two neighbouring cattle enclosures, both of which may have been made by the peaceful settlers of the New Forest Potteries.

THE ANCIENT EARTHWORKS OF THE NEW FOREST, 30–33

EARTHWORK IN ANSES

Although this earthwork may be termed minimus rather than minor, it is worth noting. It is situated in most beautiful woodland scenery on the northern side of the Forest, and may be found at the lower western end of Anses, beside the track leading up to Ocknell Plain. A magnificent beech (of which the moss-grown bole is shown in the drawing), grows on the northern corner of this enclosure. The site is on the side of a hill which slopes gently down to the upper Dockens Water. The soil is sandy clay. The overall measurement of bank and ditch is about 12 feet. The bank rises about 1 foot above the ditch, and 6 inches above the area. It is spread and consolidated, but continuously defined except on the western side—where presumably was the entrance. The ditch is silted up with leaf mould. The area measures 40 feet by 27 feet.

This little earthwork has to be sought for in order to be found, for it is somewhat overgrown, and it is the smallest in dimension of area, and in section of bank and ditch of any earthwork herein recorded. It does not belong to the "Bee-garden" type of enclosure; in size, it is larger; and in situation, it is too remote from the forest boundaries—Bee-gardens were made for the usage of dwellers on the edge of the forest—while its bank and ditch are different both in condition and profile to those of Bee-gardens. I think that it is ancient, and conjecture that it may belong to the pastoral type which we have been considering. The value of mast feed in the Forest was assessed when Domesday was compiled, from which we may infer that it was then an established practice to turn out pigs in the Forest in the autumn. Possibly this small enclosure was originally made as a pound to protect mast-feeding swine at night.

The beauty of Anses wood is notable. It is also remarkable for many curious examples of ingrowth which may be seen here. Beech and holly are the trees that most frequently develop this vagary, and the sketches given will suggest the

Old Beech standing on the N. corner of the Earthwork

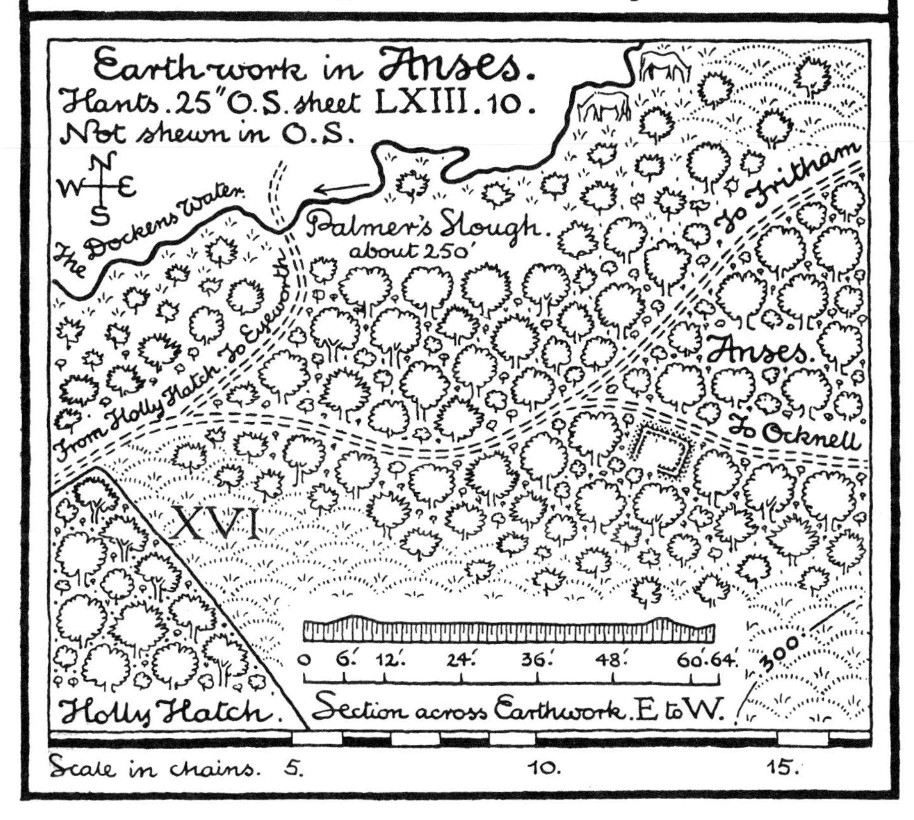

contorted shapes which result from the will-to-grow of untended saplings, struggling upwards, successfully, in spite of obstructions, until in time they amalgamate into unwonted stems and ramifications, and assume strange forms.

THE ANCIENT EARTHWORKS OF THE NEW FOREST, 66–8

NOTABLE BARROWS

Disc barrows are most beautiful forms of ancient earthwork, and the twin disc barrows on Setley Plain have the unusual distinction of being united by the intersection of their encircling banks. The three disc barrows shown in Plan XXII are the only examples of this type that I have found in the New Forest district. They are rare in Hampshire, but a group of five may be seen in close proximity on Oakley Down, Cranborne Chase, Dorset, while there are many on the downs round Stonehenge in Wilts. The sections below are fairly typical of the disc barrows on Oakley Down, and of those near Stonehenge. The similarity of their type is remarkable, and their difference in over-all measurements to these on Setley Plain is also remarkable.

There is another difference between these New Forest disc barrows and those mentioned above. One rather large mound rises in the middle of the encircled areas on Setley Plain, while in the Dorset and Wilts examples the central mound is quite small, and is often flanked by a second mound, and sometimes by a third—presumably subsequent interments within a sacred area.

In 1792 Richard Warner dug holes in these disc barrows on Setley Plain, and thus introduces an account of his wrong-doing in *Topographical Remarks*, p. 60: "It may be amusing to spend a few minutes in contemplating these repositories of the departed warriors, and in offering some observations on this very ancient mode of interment." The observations may be spared, but there is something to be learnt from the following brief record, p. 73: "*Cremation* had obviously been practised; since large quantities of burnt earth, and parcels of wood reduced by fire to charcoal, were found in each: but after searching with great attention, removing all the factitious earth, and digging to a considerable depth below the surface of the natural land, we were convinced that simply burning the body, and covering its ashes with mould, had been the mode observed in these instances of inhumation."

From the present appearance of these mounds, Richard Warner's excavations seem to have been made by means of digging holes from the top downwards, and he showed his deficient appreciation of the beauty of these earthworks by not filling in his excavations. In the plan I have not indicated such random holes, but have taken their present edges as representing the top of the central mounds.

Barrows truly express "earth to earth" in monumental form. Reverence, and commemoration are our only clues to the religious tradition that ordered their making; but we may recognize ritual significance in their construction, for the precision of their circular alignment is in sharp contrast with the irregularity of the defensive and pastoral earthworks made during the same period. Centuries of

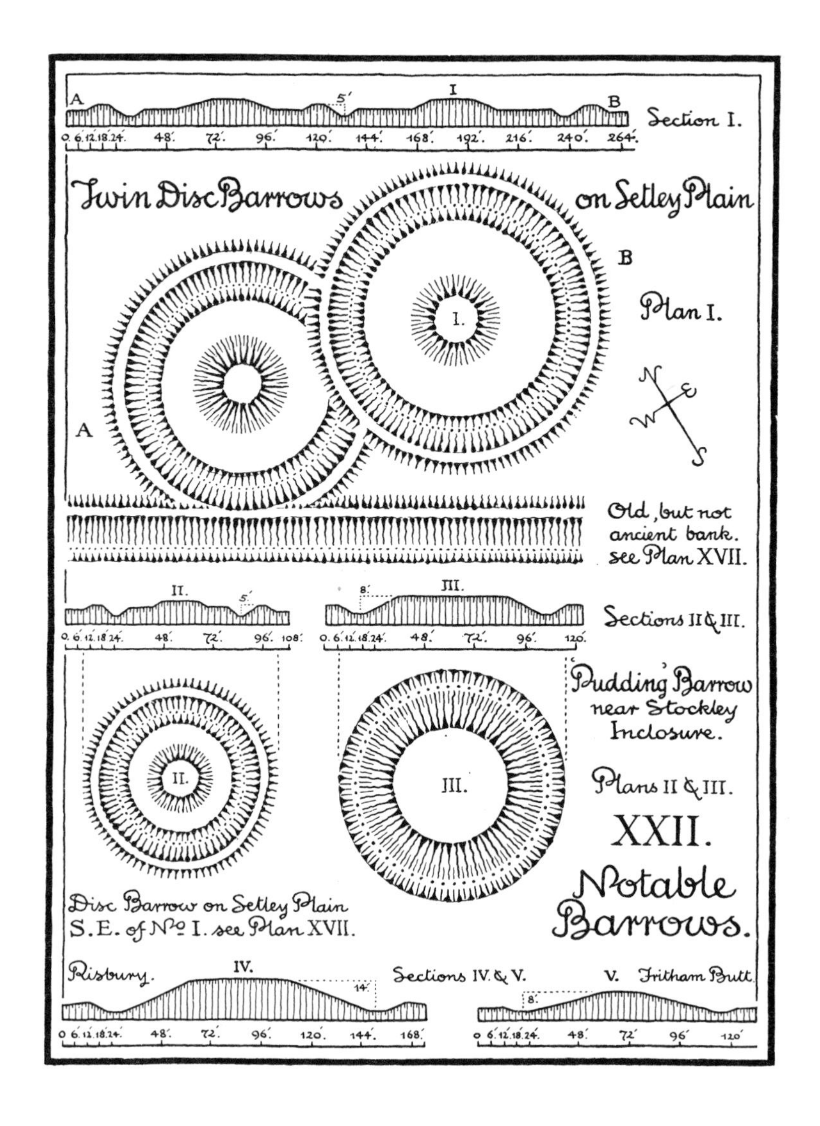
Section I.
Twin Disc Barrows on Setley Plain
Plan I.
Old, but not ancient bank. see Plan XVII.
Sections II & III.
'Pudding' Barrow near Stockley Inclosure.
Plans II & III.
XXII.
Notable Barrows.
Disc Barrow on Setley Plain S.E. of No I. see Plan XVII.
Risbury.
Sections IV. & V.
V. Fritham Butt

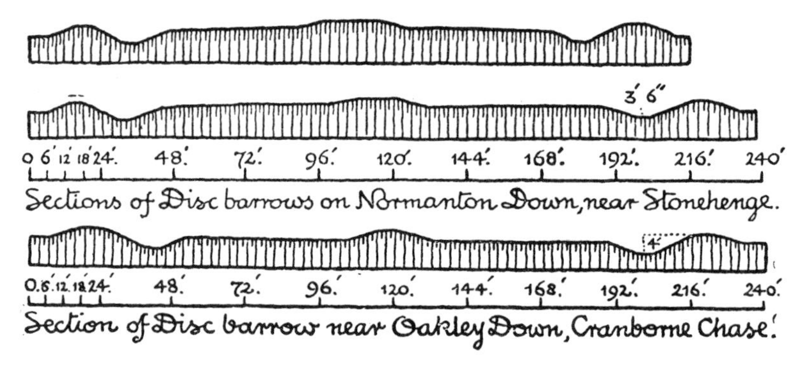
Sections of Disc barrows on Normanton Down, near Stonehenge.
Section of Disc barrow near Oakley Down, Cranborne Chase.

heath bells have bloomed and withered on the Forest plains since these barrows were first raised; and as the centuries have multiplied, oblivion has supervened, until now "the Butts" abide merely as natural landmarks—daily passed by with little thought of their primitive significance. Yet such neglect does not destroy. Perhaps we should almost praise neglect as an ignorant form of preservation. Certainly curiosity and random hole digging have wrought more damage to New Forest barrows than have the wastage and neglect of all the intervening centuries.

THE ANCIENT EARTHWORKS OF THE NEW FOREST, 80–83

THE OLD "HEDGE OF RIDLEY COPPICE"

The differences between the forester and the forest lover are difficult to adjust. The forester regards trees as a crop, to be grown and sold to the best advantage. The forest lover looks on, admires the wild growth, and ruin and renewal of the old woods, but regards inclosure with aversion. The forester says that the present wild beauty of the old woods—such as Ridley and Mark Ash—is due to original inclosure when these "coppices" were set with oak and beech 300 years ago, and urges re-inclosure as the best means to protect the self-sown renewals of these old woods from the destructive nibbling of ponies and cattle. Surely in these contentions he is right. But granting this, he cannot persuade the forest lover to expect that similar beauty will eventually arise within the modern inclosures of Scots pine. Stray woodland undergrowth does not thrive under trees which shed pine needles; they are good to walk on, and to smell, but nothing grows in their resinous litter. A gardener values a cartload of leaf-mould, but has no use for pine needles; and the chance-come seedlings and the climbing plants agree with the gardener—they refuse to grow beneath a canopy of Scots pine. Birch seems to be the only tree that is willing to fill up the gaps in such plantations. In old age Scots pine may be very beautiful, either singly or planted in clumps, but they become monotonous when multiplied in a plantation. Their habit of growth is unvaried and without power of self-heal. They do not effectively repair mischance, as do their deciduous forest brethren. Still, now more than ever, timber must be grown to the best advantage, and if Scots pine is the most paying forest crop, we must accept it. Forest beauty has come by chance in the past, and perhaps the present regularity and sameness of the modern inclosures may be modified and gradually changed by some future natural chance that we cannot now anticipate. It is useless for the forest lover to gird at inclosures; and when we hear the clang of their well-hung gates behind us as we enter their monotonous rides, we must imagine—imagine the woodland changes and chances of centuries ahead.

The future beauty of the modern inclosures may be doubtful, but the present beauty of the old woods is sure. In the old woods of oak and beech and holly each tree tells a tale of growth, of mishaps, and of renewals—different episodes in the forest struggle for life. Woody knobs and cushions gnarl their trunks, telling of branch loss, of bark repair, of wood wounds and of sap bleeding. Deep dints in the old boles mark some hidden obstruction to outward growth, or some windfall bruise. Branches cross and ingrow with an overlap of cambium bark that marks the self-heal of the woods. Suckers spring up awry, and bury themselves in the parent stem. Moss and lichen, honeysuckle and travellers' joy clothe trunks and limbs, while butchers' broom and strange toad-stools grow in the crotches of the roots. These old woods hold the spell of magic. In their shades there is a good smell of timber, of fallen leaves, and of heather. Stray sounds of creaking boughs, of brown owls hooting, of tapping woodpeckers, of harsh jays and amid these sights and scents and sounds the curious seeker will find the wasted mediaeval earthwork (*circa* 1570), that marks the old "hedge" of Ridley "coppice."

The plan shows the line of this inclosure bank and ditch, which delimits an area of about fifty acres. It may be traced continuously in spite of being wasted and broken about in places. It compares in construction and in alignment with the bank and ditch that surround Sloden hill-top inclosure, and the purpose fulfilled by such old enclosures is thus described in *A brief History of the Arboriculture of the New Forest, Hampshire*, by the Honble. Gerald Lascelles, late Deputy Surveyor. "The practice of cultivation seems to have been that of 'natural regeneration,' such as is advocated by the most distinguished foresters of the modern school. In old days it went by the name of 'encoppicing,' and the process seems to have been simply to enclose the area of a fence against cattle and deer, and to rely on the natural reproduction of the seed from the existing crop of trees to replenish the wood. After the coppice was fairly established, it seems to have been the practice to farm it out on lease for a term of years."

Many of the old trees in Ridley wood have been pollarded—or "shrouded" as it was called in the presentments of the regarders of the Forest in the sixteenth century. The life of man is too short for exact knowledge to be established in arboriculture. The finest results seem to come by chance—as here, where the illegal "shrouding of 200 trees in the said coppice" (Ridley), followed by their subsequent protection and free growth has resulted in the present beauty of Ridley wood. We need the span of Methuselah, and the observation of Gilbert White, or of his friend Robert Marsham, in order to know whether the life of trees is prolonged by early pollarding. Many of the finest old trees in the forest are pollards, and we now profit by the original misdeeds of the sixteenth century "shrouders."

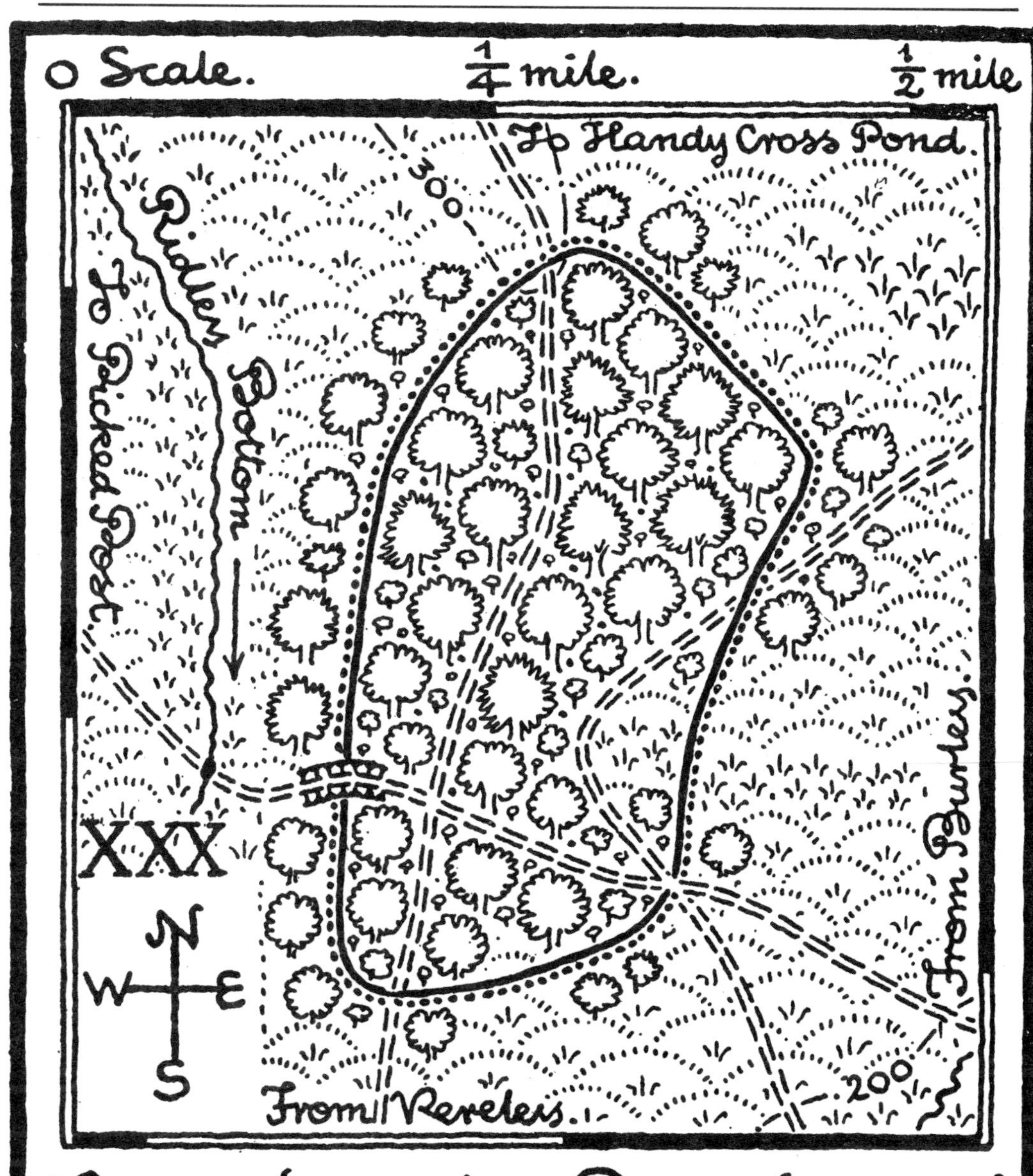

The old 'hedge' of Ridley 'Coppice'
Hants. 6 inch sheet LXXI. S.W.
.... The line = bank. The dots = ditch

The Western Entrance of Ridley 'Coppice'. H.S. 1914.

The approach from Ridley bottom to this old inclosure, passes up a hollow way that is deeply sunk in the bluff on the western side of Ridley wood. This way has been worn by forest traffic, and by the scour of rainwash, channelling sandy soil. It is shown in the headpiece, and the old inclosure bank and ditch cross this hollow way about 8 feet above its present level. This sunken and secluded trackway was used for secret trafficking in the smuggling days. There is authentic tradition in Burley of this site having been the meeting-place for forest customers of the smugglers' "run"; and "smugglers' road"—crossing the heath from Crow—marks their line of access from the Avon Valley.

THE ANCIENT EARTHWORKS OF THE NEW FOREST, 114–7

SALTERNS ON KEYHAVEN MARSHES NEAR LYMINGTON

A survey of the earthworks in the New Forest district would be incomplete without some mention of the derelict salterns and of the sea-banks which may be found along the shore of the Solent. These earthworks are *old*, not *ancient*, and they have been wasted by neglect, cut about by latter-day requirements, and rendered useless by further reclamation of the sea-marshes in which they are situated.

Three salt-pans are recorded along this coast in the Hampshire Domesday

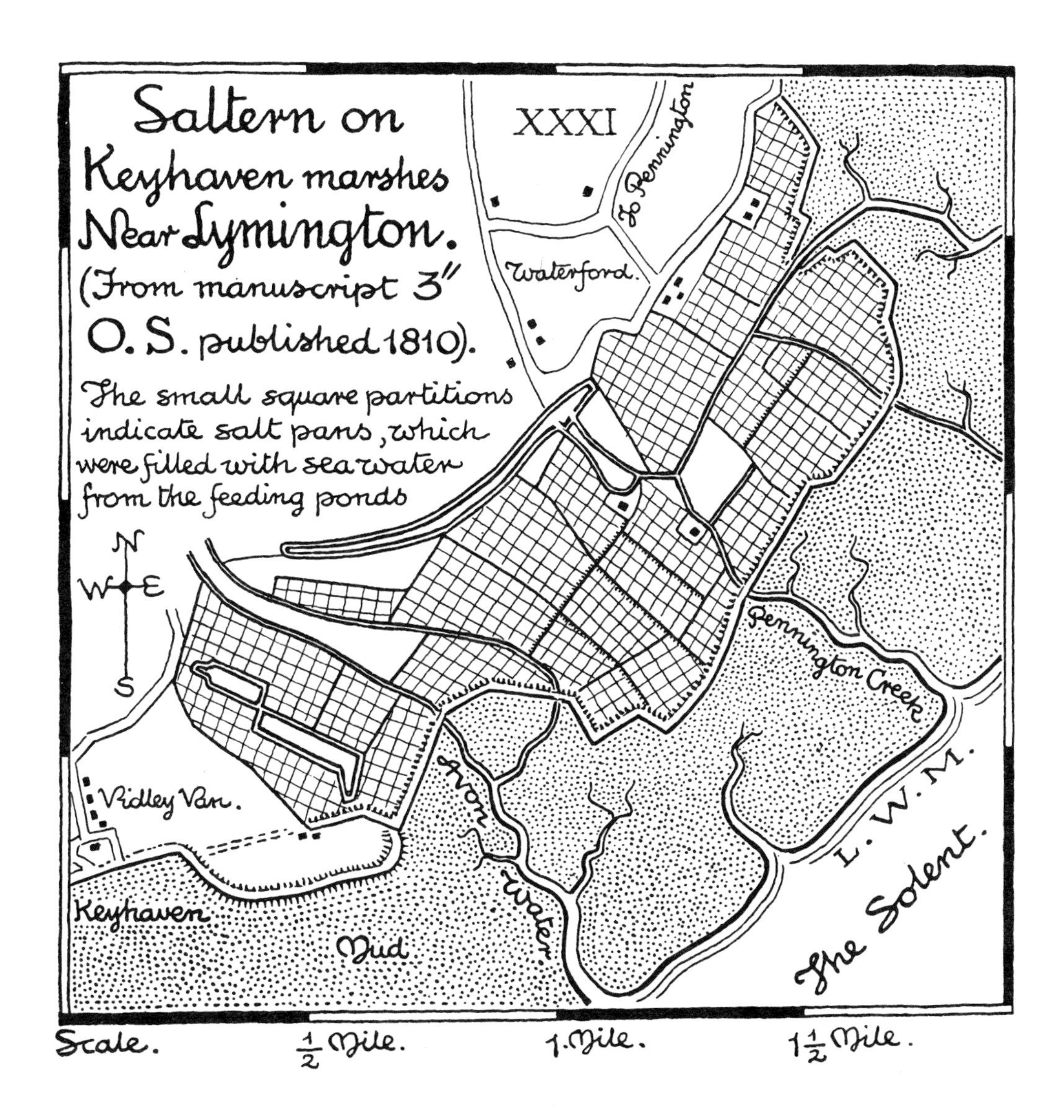

survey. Namely, at *Edlinges* (Eling), "a fishery and a salt-pan without profit." At *Depedene* (Dibden), "a salt-pan and a fishery." And at *Herdel* (Hordle), "There are a mill and salt-pans worth 15 pence." The salt-pans at *Lentune* (Lymington), must have been worked soon after Domesday date (1086–87), for in 1147 Richard de Redvers granted a tithe of all the salt-works of *Limentoniae* to the Abbey of Quarre, in the Isle of Wight.

Salinarii, i.e., men working on salterns are recorded in several entries of the Dorset Domesday survey, but no *Salinarii* are mentioned in the Hampshire survey, an omission that seems to imply that the Dorest salterns were of more importance than these in Hampshire when Domesday was compiled—a superiority which they did not afterwards retain.

The salterns along the shore of the Solent were worked with profit until the beginning of the nineteenth century. It is said that the Lymington salt-works paid as much as £50,000 a year duty to the Exchequer at their most prosperous period in the eighteenth century. Competition, and lack of coal near by eventually caused the decay of this local industry. The former traffic inland of the manufactured salt is testified by the Saltway place-names recorded in the boundaries of the Manor of Lyndhurst.

There is a good account of the methods employed in these salterns in Vancouver's *Agriculture of Hampshire* (p. 120), of which the following is a brief summary: The sea-water was first admitted to the feeding ponds, thence it flowed into open pans to the depth of about 3 inches. These pans were about 20 to 30 square perches in size (*i.e.* 8 to 5⅓ pans to an acre), and were lined with plates of wrought iron. Thus exposed to wind and sun the brine became of sufficient strength to be pumped into boiling pans, in which the salt was finally dried by artificial heat. The industry could only be pursued during the summer months, and a dry spell was needful for successful results.

These salterns have now reverted to furzey marsh land, broken by irregular pools, which mark the feeding ponds, and brimming ditches, which mark the conduits to the salt-pans. But the sea-banks—earthwork land-ward, rough stone wall sea-ward—remain much the same as shown in the plan; with the exception of a sea sluice-gate, erected in 1859, to regulate the outflow of the Avon Water.

THE ANCIENT EARTHWORKS OF THE NEW FOREST, 117–8

THE SOLITARY DIGGER

SUMNER THE ARCHAEOLOGIST

Sumner's career as an excavating archaeologist began in 1911 when he was 58 years old and continued without a break until, at the age of 72, having examined no less than 13 sites, he retired from the field. It was an impressive achievement, not least when it is remembered that for much of the time he worked by himself (though occasionally with a few labourers) and that everything he found was meticulously and speedily published.

The world of archaeology in the early decades of this century was very simple, and much more leisurely than it is today. General Pitt-Rivers, working on his estates in Cranborne Chase, had set high standards of recording and publication in the 1880s but few had followed him. The Society of Antiquaries' excavations at the Roman towns of Silchester and Caerwent, though extensive, were conducted to a much lower standard. But in 1910/11 the Society initiated a new programme of excavation, beginning at Hengistbury Head, under the direction of J. P. Bushe-Fox, whose techniques of digging and recording showed a marked advance on his predecessors (though were still no match for Pitt-Rivers). It was natural, then, for Sumner, who had had no archaeological training, to look to the works of Pitt-Rivers for guidance and inspiration. Significantly it is Pitt-Rivers he quotes at the beginning of his first excavation report on Rockbourne Down.

> There are people who think they are doing good by digging and grubbing out antiquities, without making any record at all of their investigations. . . . A discovery dates only from the time of the record of it, and not from the time of its being found in the soil.

Needless to say he followed his master's example faithfully, working slowly, recording everything he discovered with great care, and publishing his results in detail within months of finishing the excavation.

The excavations of the Romano-British enclosure were to last from 1911 until the spring of 1913, the excavation report being published in the next year. Meanwhile he had begun to explore the Roman villa near East Grimstead in the valley of the Dean Brook—assisted, on this occasion, by three labourers. But the difficulties caused by the First World War began to make themselves felt and after a brief spring season he suspended operations. Work was eventually resumed in June 1922 and continued each summer until August 1924. Again with remarkable rapidity the report was published by the end of the year.

The First World War saw Sumner heavily involved within his local community in voluntary work for the war effort and shortage of manpower meant that excavation was difficult. Nonetheless, as a lone worker, he persisted, examining a number of sites in the New Forest within easy reach of his home—the earthwork known as Sloden Churchyard in 1915, the enclosure on Gorley Hill in 1916 and four of the barrows on Ibsley Common in 1917.

It was in December 1917 that he began his investigation of the Roman pottery kilns of the New Forest—work for which he is best known among archaeologists. The kiln sites had been known for some time, but early excavation by Bartlett and Wise were little better than treasure hunts designed to produce collections of pottery. Sumner was more imaginative. As a good practical man he wanted to understand the technology of Roman pottery production, and as an archaeologist he wished to study the way of life of the potters. This meant systematic excavation on a comparatively large scale.

His first excavations were at Ashley Rails, where from December 1917 until October 1918 he averaged about five days a month of solitary digging. His efforts were rewarded by the discovery of three ill-preserved kilns and a considerable quantity of decorated pottery. In 1919 he was examining Crock Hills and Black Heath Meadow. In 1920 he moved to Old Sloden Wood and Sloden Enclosure before going back to Black Heath Meadow, this time using a party of boys from Taunton School. This work was on a more extended scale and yielded plans of five well-preserved kilns together with considerable quantities of the pottery they had produced.

In spring 1922 he returned to the southern part of Black Heath Meadow where another kiln was excavated. A chance discovery drew him back to the Forest in 1925, this time to Islands Thorns, where for eight days he examined a potter's hut. His final campaign, a further eight-day session in June 1925, saw him excavating another kiln, at Rough Piece, Linwood.

His work on the New Forest pottery kilns had occupied much of his field-work effort from December 1917 to November 1920 and rather less time in the spring of 1922 and the spring and summer of 1925. His results were, of course, fully published. Two short monographs in 1919 and 1921 were brought together and supplemented with the later work in a book—*Excavations in New Forest Roman Pottery Sites*, published in 1927—which has remained and will continue to remain a standard work on the subject. It is Sumner the archaeologist at his best: thoughtful observation and careful recording of the excavated structures together with a thorough illustration of all the finds.

His New Forest pottery work and the completion of the East Grimstead villa occupied most of the post-war period until 1925, but in 1921 he spent a few days completing his barrow excavations on Ibsley Common and in late spring and early summer undertook some trial trenching at the Iron Age hillfort at Dudsbury in the Stour Valley. The completion of the kiln excavation at Linwood in June 1925 marked the end of his excavating activities (with the exception of the rescue excavation of a mammoth tusk found in gravel working in Ibsley Park in 1930). At the age of 72 he could gracefully retire.

As an archaeologist Sumner was not an innovator nor did his work add significantly to the development of British archaeology. He chose to work on a small scale, usually alone, and thus his contribution was correspondingly small scale, but everything he did he did well: his excavation reports are perfect vignettes, exuding the enthusiasm of youthful old age. Alone in his beloved New Forest with his spade and with problems to solve, Sumner was in his element and with the trees as companions he could ask for nothing more.

EXCAVATION OF BARROWS ON IBSLEY COMMON

Ibsley Common is a detached outlier of the ridge that apparently once stretched from Fritham to Mockbeggar. It is 1½ miles in length, 1 mile in width, and contains 887 acres. It rises to a height of 257 feet above the sea, and of 180 feet above the Avon, and on every side its plateau gravel summit terminates in salient bluffs above the surrounding valleys.

The plan shows the salient and retiring contours of the 200 foot line—above which lies the plateau gravel capping. Below this is a bed of sand, in some places white, in others yellow. The only section available—on the North side of Cuckoo Hill—indicates a thickness of 15 to 20 feet. The sand rests upon clay that holds up and yields the surface water in springs that ooze out along the flanks of these bluffs. The tilt of this clay subsoil appears to be downward from North-West to South-East, for the spring water comes out of the hillsides much higher above the Hucklesbrook valley than above the Dockenswater.

The ridge summit above and between the 200 foot contours is called "the plain," and at Whitefield the terrace levels are well displayed, which mark the gradual erosion of the Avon valley. The soil is very poor—heath, scattered furze rakes and bracken cover this expanse, the latter marking the folds of the hills and leading down to boggy bottoms matted with sphagnum moss, scented with sweet gale and starred in summer with tufts of cotton grass and spikes of yellow bog asphodel. These re-entering folds of the hill are locally called "drokes." Spacious views over three counties—Hampshire, Dorset, and Wiltshire—may be

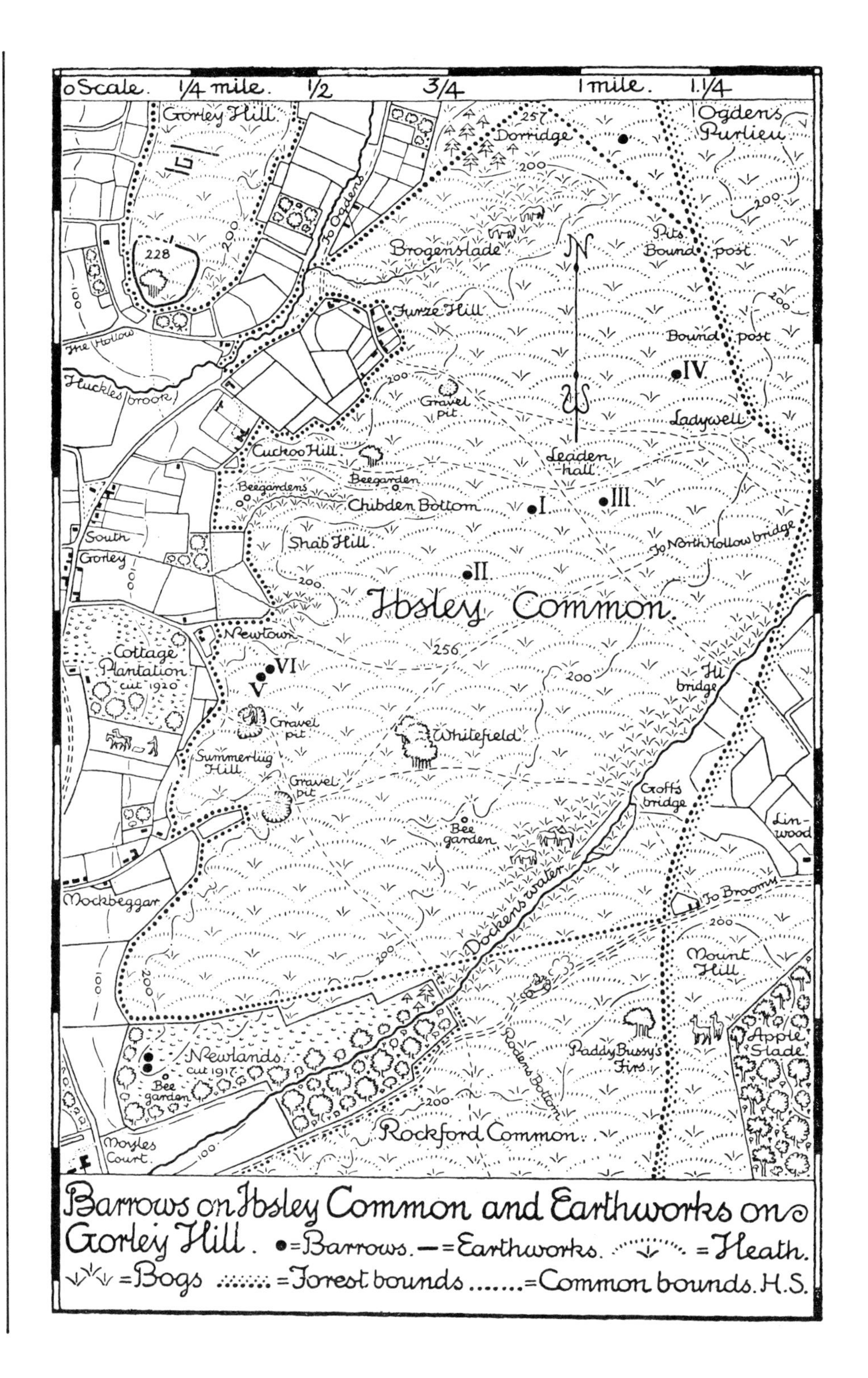

Barrows on Ibsley Common and Earthworks on Gorley Hill. •=Barrows. —=Earthworks. = Heath. =Bogs =Forest bounds ....=Common bounds. H.S.

seen from the plains of Ibsley Common, and on the hottest days of summer breezes from the distant sea or from the chalk downs refresh the air that quivers above the heath; but year in and year out the heath-bells bloom and wither with few to see their weeks of midsummer splendour, or their months of sober vesture.

The common abides in solitude, only broken by vagrant stock, by herdsman, turf-cutter or gravel-digger, or by Linwood children on their way to and from school at South Gorley. Yet once upon a time these plains were chosen for special distinction. Here barrows were laboriously raised to commemorate the dead. Here remote ritual and assembly were held. Here was a site worthy of monumental reverence. Beneath the heath and fern-clad plains of Ibsley Common lies the scanty prehistoric evidence which we seek to discover and interpret.

The following record describes the results obtained by excavation in these barrows by kind permission of the Lord of the Manor—Lord Normanton. In every instance the barrow has been restored to its former profile.

Solitary excavation was imposed by the necessities of the times. It is a slow and laborious process, with only one compensation, namely, the excavator knows every spit of soil up-turned. Thus he may be helped to an exact estimation of finds and of barrow-soil origin and deposition. The solitary digger should obtain all the evidence communicable by prong and spade. The spells of mere labour—such as preliminary trenching, soil removal, and the final filling in—must be accepted as drudgery in the pursuit of knowledge.

Barrow No. 1 (May 1917), not shown in the Ordnance Survey, is a small disc barrow of unusual type. The central mound rises from the scarp edge of the inside ditch instead of from an intervening space of level area, and the "over-all" measurement of the whole earthwork is only 50 feet. I do not know of any disc barrow that compares with this one.

A trench 6 feet wide was dug from South to North across the ditch on both sides, which revealed a shallow V-shaped ditch, the bottom being 1 foot 2 inches below the top surface. Nothing was found in the filling. The trench was increased to 9 feet in width as it entered the mound, which was made of gravel and sandy mould obtained from near by. About 6 inches to the West of the centre and 1 foot 2 inches below the top surface burnt matter was found surrounding an inverted urn; the latter was gradually uncovered, and proved to be standing in a small cist, 1 foot 6 inches by 1 foot 4 inches, and 8 inches in depth, cut in the undisturbed gravel subsoil, and floored with rammed pebble-stones. The cist was filled with black, unctuous burnt matter, interspersed with charcoal, but no burnt bones were found. The little urn was in a very rotten condition, pierced and broken by heath roots and quite impossible to handle. Accordingly, after clearing out the

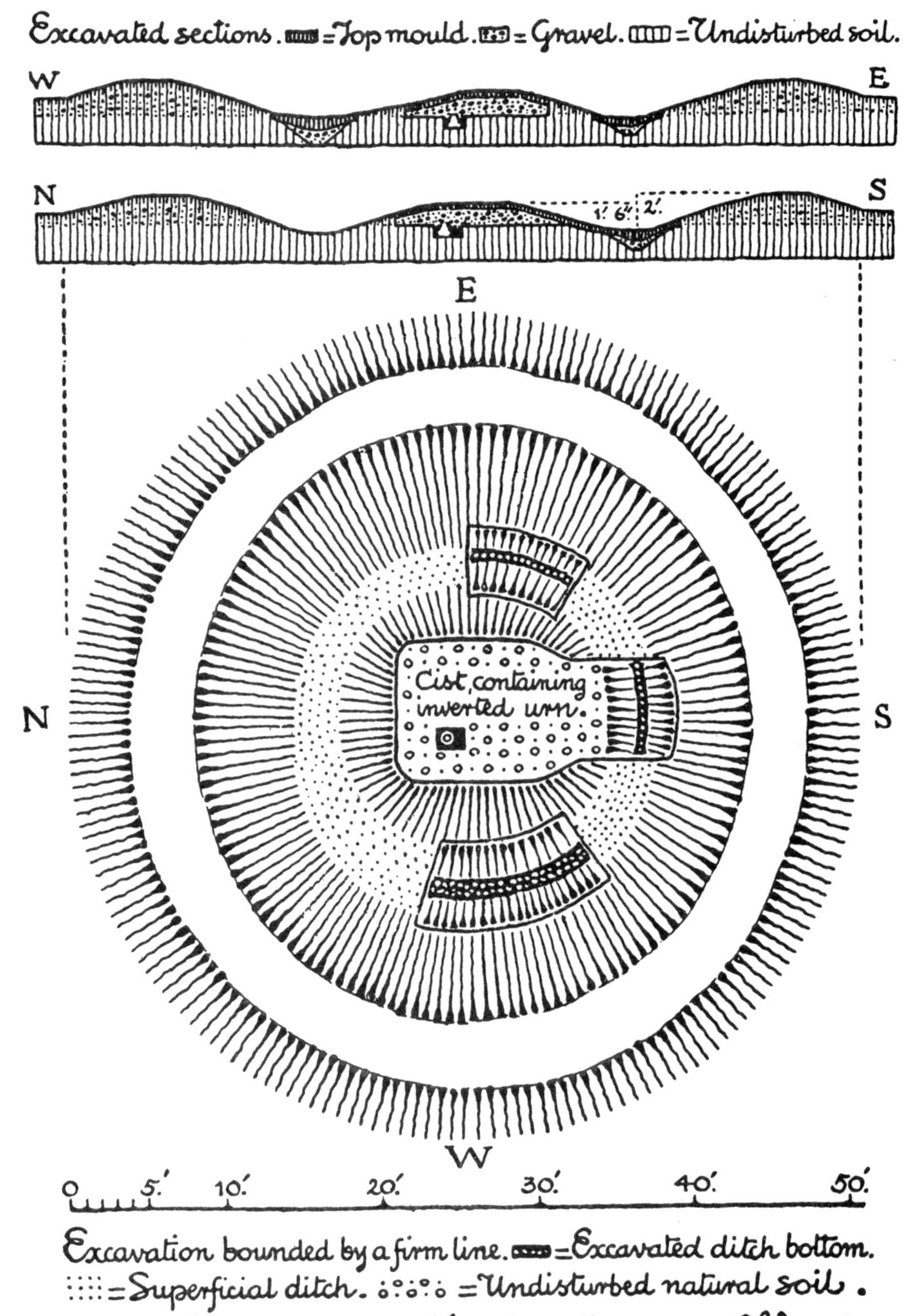

Disc barrow on Ibsley Common Hants
no I.

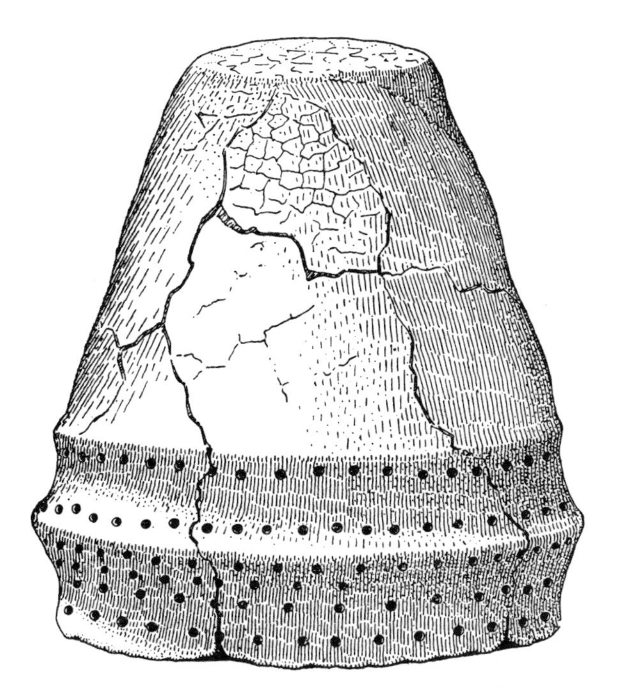

Urn of cinerary type, from a disc barrow on Ibsley Common Hants.

surrounding burnt matter in the cist, the urn was left to dry, roofed over with tools supporting clots. The weather was favourable—sunny and windy. After two days' interval the mouth of the urn was severed from the ashes on which it stood and to which it adhered, and was then safely removed.

Nothing was found inside the urn except fine mould which had filtered in through the cracks made by the heath roots, and burnt matter which filled its inverted mouth.

This urn has been restored, and may be seen at the Salisbury Museum. It is 6.03 inches in height, 5.05 inches in width at the mouth, and 2.06 inches at the base.

The absence of any bones in the burnt matter cannot be explained by their disappearance from decay. This burial may express formular recognition of the rite of cremation, *e.g.*, the burnt matter surrounding the urn; and such instances are not uncommon; they give rise to the question whether in some cases barrows have been raised as cenotaphs, or memorials of the dead who have been buried or burnt elsewhere; a question on which archaeologists disagree.

Further excavation yielded no discovery except that the ditch was wider and deeper on the Western side of the circle than elsewhere—presumably in order to provide additional material, either for the central mound or for the encircling bank.

The circle of this bank was struck with precision, and it is evenly wasted and consolidated. The inside ditch is continuous—according to its superficial appearance. Prehistoric man was wont to make his ditch against the enemy he feared, *outside* the defensive bank. The *inside* ditch of disc barrows may indicate that the living feared the dead, and dreaded their return.

LOCAL PAPERS, 108–113

THE ROMANO-BRITISH ENCLOSURE ON ROCKBOURNE DOWN

At the eastern end of Spring Pond the mounds by which it is surrounded are joined by low earthworks of a different type. A well defined bank between two slight ditches runs South-East for 19 yards, and then after a gap of 5 yards, continues with the same section for 14 yards, here the construction changes, the bank becomes broader and lower, and is flanked by mere depressions on either side (the inner being the larger) that mark silted up ditches—the bank being about 15 feet across, and from 1 to 2 feet 6 inches high. A few yards farther on this broad bank turns a rounded corner, and runs North-East to a thorn brake 448 yards distant. Here, after a gap of 20 yards, there is an offshoot branch pointing due north which runs for 40 yards across the down valley with a section resembling the bank that joins Spring Pond, it then becomes broad and low as before, but with only one ditch apparent—on the western or area side of the bank. The main bank of the enclosure likewise changes its construction at the thorn brake aforesaid, and continues both narrower and higher in section for 90 yards, when, before reaching a small dry pond, it turns Northward, now again becoming broad and low, but with only one ditch apparent—on the North-Eastern, or outside of the Enclosure, and thus it joins the offshoot branch described above, 120 yards from the corner near the dry pond. After this junction, the entrenchment resumes its usual construction, and thus it runs up the slope towards the North for 600 yards. Then it makes a gradual, rounded curve, and becomes broader and better defined for 110 yards, after which, all trace of the earthwork is lost in cultivation. It reappears on the South-Eastern side of Down Barn, and continues for 400 yards until again it is lost in cultivation pointing towards the North-Western side of Spring Pond.

The area enclosed by this Entrenchment amounts to about 96 acres. The land slopes about 80 feet in half a mile from North to South, and within the circuit of the earthwork is included a shallow valley, down which a constant stream probably flowed in Romano-British times. It lies on the lower chalk slopes that trend Southward from the Oxdrove Ridgeway towards the Avon valley, and it was probably in open country then, as now. The small number of roe-deer bones found during my excavations support this conjecture. To the West, the far distance is bounded by the hill-top trees that mark the site of Ashmore; to the North, by Knighton Wood, New Farm, and Great Yews; to the East, by Standlynch, Redlynch, and Bramshaw Telegraph; and to the South, by Damerham Knoll, Martin Wood, and Pentridge.

Three questions are suggested by this preliminary description. When was this Enclosure made? For what purpose was it made? And was Spring Pond a feature in its original construction?

Excavation has given the answer to the first question, namely—During the third century A.D. And also to the second, namely—for a Farm Enclosure, abundant evidence both of cattle, and of corn, were found in the course of the excavations. As to the third question, it seems hardly probable that Spring Pond was a feature in the original construction of this Enclosure. When General Pitt-Rivers excavated the Romano-British village at Woodcuts, about 9 miles distant, he found a dry Roman well with a bucket at the bottom, showing that formerly it had been in use as a well. Comparison with existing wells in that neighbourhood indicated that the water level must have sunk considerably since the time when this Roman well held water, the difference in the present water levels, and in the bottom of the Roman well ranging from 12 feet to 101 feet. Accordingly, if this were the case here on Rockbourne Down, and if we estimate the sinking of the water level at, say, 50 feet, there would have been a constant stream flowing down the valley, and through the Enclosure 1600 years ago, and a pond would not have been needed. It seems probable that the original Spring Pond, and its subsequent deepening, mark the need caused by the lowering water-level of the chalk springs, but this must have happened centuries after the time when this pastoral enclosure was first entrenched by the Romanized Britons.

After making such survey as I have described and planned, my observations were directed to the Down land that still remains uncultivated within the area of this large enclosure. Signs of Habitation—humps and hollows, with potsherds on the mole-hills and rabbit scrapes were found on the upper, North-Eastern side of the area, and here, helped by the experience and advice of Colonel Hawley, who kindly came over from Old Sarum to inspect the site, I began to excavate in 1911. The place chosen was a hollow on the Down where moles and rabbits worked freely, and threw up potsherds. Excavation proved this to be a roughly dug refuse pit in which nothing was found but sherds and a few iron nails.

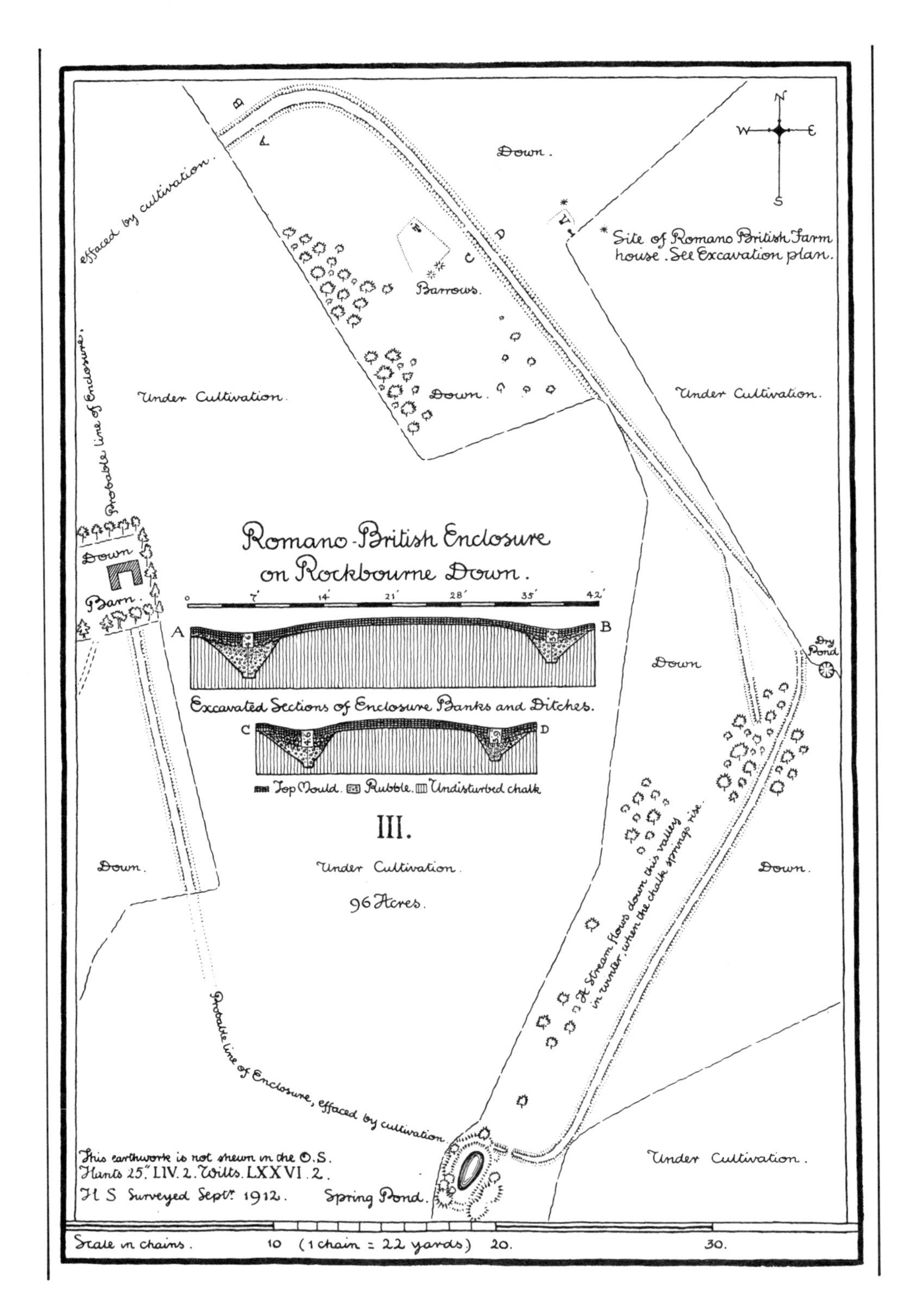

Romano-British Enclosure on Rockbourne Down.
0 7' 14' 21' 28' 35' 42'
A
B
Excavated Sections of Enclosure Banks and Ditches.
C
D
Top Mould. Rubble. Undisturbed chalk
III.
Under Cultivation.
96 Acres.
Down.
Barrows.
Under Cultivation.
Down.
Under Cultivation.
effaced by cultivation,
Probable line of Enclosure,
Down
Barn.
* Site of Romano British Farm house. See Excavation plan.
Dry Pond
Down
Down.
Down.
A Stream flows down this valley in winter when the chalk springs rise.
Probable line of Enclosure, effaced by cultivation.
Under Cultivation.
This earthwork is not shewn in the O.S. Hants 25." LIV. 2. Wilts. LXXVI. 2.
H S Surveyed Sept. 1912.
Spring Pond.
Scale in chains. 10 (1 chain = 22 yards) 20. 30.

The results of this excavation indicate a type of a peaceful pastoral and agricultural Farm site occupied by the Romanized Britons. Varro would have called it a villa, for he specially claims this name as belonging to a Farm-house, rather than to a luxuriously planned Country Mansion—which latter meaning we generally ascribe to the word. The coins found date from A.D. 253 to 375. Judging from the bones found, the stock kept consisted principally of cattle and horses, some sheep, few pigs, and dogs complete the list of domestic animals. Roe-deer and oysters provided occasional food. The wheat grown was of about the same sample in size of grain as that now grown on the same land. That Eve span when Adam delved on Rockbourne Down, is shown by the various spindle-whorl finds; and that games were played, by the pottery counters. The large number of cooking stones scattered all over this site show the method used by the inhabitants to heat water, *i.e.*, by dropping red-hot flints into wooden troughs, or into skins containing water—for they had no vessels that would stand direct heating on a fire.

Most of their pottery came from the New Forest kilns at Pitts Wood, Crock Hill, Islands Thorns, and Sloden, where may still be found a great variety of potsherds ranging from the thin, hard "thumb-pot" type, to the coarsest wheel-turned hardware. It seems probable that some of their coarse handmade ware was made on the spot, as it appears to be too soft to have travelled. Many of the fragments were pierced for suspension, possibly in order to preserve the contents of the pots from mice—for the cat does not seem to have been included in their list of domestic animals. No cat bones have been unearthed on the Romano-British sites of Cranborne Chase. Many also of the bottoms of the pots were perforated, sometimes very roughly after the vessels had been baked, and several fragments of colanders further testified to straining in the preparation of their food. General Pitt-Rivers ascribed the frequency of perforated vessels to the straining of honeycomb. Samian ware, iron nails, and a few hooks were found here and there all along the flint-filled ditch, but none were found after the flint-filling ceased. I suppose these sides of the drain ditch quadrangle to have been occupied by wattle and mortar huts (arranged in humble imitation of the Roman villa courtyard type), of which nothing has survived except the nails that were used in the wooden construction, and the varied finds before mentioned suggestive of habitation.

The water supply for the dwellers in this settlement would probably have been obtained from the upper head springs of the Spring Pond stream, supposing water to have then been flowing down the valley about 200 yards North-East of Hypocaust No. II. The cattle would have had a plentiful supply within the Enclosure at the South-East end.

To sum up, this site was a Farm Settlement of the Romano-British period. In plan, Roman, not British. The firm lines of the outer enclosure entrenchments, with their steady curve at the angle turns; their precise setting out, and cutting; and also that of the drain ditch round Hypocaust No. I quarter; the plans and the masonry of the three Hypocausts—all these assert the "Romanization of Roman Britain." And there are no signs of a pre-Roman settlement on this site—no rectification of rambling earthworks such as mark a British village. We seem to have here an example of the sort of habitation, and the size of a farm-enclosure during the most peaceful period of the Roman occupation. No defences against raiders seem to have been required. Both the site and the entrenchments, with their principal ditch and their stockade on the inside, denote the peaceful purpose of this large enclosure: and the small dwelling house of the settlement was safely placed outside its lines. The inhabited quarter of the site cannot be called a village—like those which Gen. Pitt-Rivers excavated at Woodyates and at Woodcuts. It was merely a Farm Settlement, occupied by poor labourers, a place of small importance, though not out of the way, *i.e.*, the way of the Roman road, which ran from old Sarum to Badbury and thence to Hamworthy and Dorchester, some two miles North of Rockbourne Down.

1. Barrow. 2. Barrow Ditch. 3. Romano-British Drain Ditch. 4. Spring Pond.
5. Duck's Nest. (Long Barrow) 6. Camp. 7. Damerham Knoll. 8. Grim's Ditch.

Digging for knowledge is a laborious process, but the zest of search, and the hope of discovery lighten the labour. Beneath our feet lie buried the relics of bygone life, hidden by the decay and accumulation of Mother Earth. Like the Sleeping Beauty of Romance they have slumbered for centuries, till, disturbed by our quest, they waken, and unfold forgotten ways of life.

An elderly gentleman digging earth with a prong is a dull substitute for the young prince cutting through a rose bower with a sword, and solving the issue with an instant kiss. Yet the upshot may compare. Excavators may also revive and recreate; they may waken sites and relics that have long been sleeping, and may give a fresh interpretation to the fable. But our results, comparatively speaking, will be poor and scanty in Britain. The beauty sleeping beneath the ancient sites of other lands arises with a splendour that, here, we shall seek for in vain. On every side of life the Ancient East surpassed the Ancient West. Still we shall not thus be deterred. We are rooted in Britain, and the past life of our own forefathers must always appeal to us in a special and intimate manner. With Touchstone, we justify our gains, such as they are.—"A poor virgin, sir, an ill-favoured thing, sir, but mine own."

EXCAVATIONS ON ROCKBOURNE DOWN, 13–15, 28–30

THE ROMAN VILLAS ALONG THE DEAN BROOK

We must follow the down-track along the ridge, through Grimstead Beeches, to a steep, bare chalk way descending the far Western flank of Dean Hill that tells white for miles beyond, seen against the grey-green down. Yews, Whitebeams, and Junipers grow on this scarp in lovely contrast, and Wayfarer's tree, Spindle, Dogwood, Ivydrums, and Thorn trees overgrown with Traveller's Joy make a tangled boundary along the lower length of the track. Then a straight drove-way between old thorn hedges leads across open, rolling, arable land, where a tractor plough can drive a mile-long furrow without turning, towards East Grimstead village—across the Southern Railway, and the derelict canal—then right-handed along the Salisbury and Dean road for a quarter of a mile, when wheels will no longer serve our purpose, so we must dismount and tramp across meadows channelled by the Dean brook (a tributary of the Test), beyond which is our site, sloping to the South, sheltered on the North by Lower Highwood Copse, and on the East by Churchway Copse.

Evidently the Roman settlers regarded the Dean brook valley as desirable for occupation. Throughout the whole area of the adjoining New Forest there has been no discovery of a Roman villa site. The Romans were good farmers, and a villa was primarily a farm. New Forest soil was not good enough, as they rightly estimated; but that of the Dean brook valley was; so here we find within a distance of three miles three villa sites, namely East Grimstead, West Dean, and Holbury, all just outside the New Forest. This sequence of villa sites beside the Dean brook, and Roman finds at Hurstbourne Priors, Wherwell, Chilbolton, Longstock, Bossington, Abbotswood, and Nursling beside the Test, indicate that these valleys were reclaimed from swamp conditions in Roman times.

The soil here is good loam, on chalk bordering Reading Beds, and the aspect is due South, about 170 feet above the sea. The land slopes gently towards the Dean brook, of which the flow here is curiously intermittent; *e.g.*, the brook may be flowing under the bridge near East Grimstead church, but be quite dry a quarter of a mile down stream, and so on for two miles, until at West Dean the brook again reappears. This happens throughout summer and autumn; in winter and spring the flow may be continuous: but whatever was the flow in Roman times, we may be sure that Roman well-sinkers had not deep to dig for their water supply. Moreover, this Dean brook valley was not then out-of-the-way according to ancient traffic-way standard, for the Roman road from Old Sarum to Winchester lay three miles distant to the North, and from Old Sarum another road led past Andover to Silchester—both town centres of Romano-British life, while the seaport of Southampton was 15 miles distant to the South-east. Towards the North and East there were many villa sites, so East Grimstead was on the verge of what must have been then "a good neighbourhood," with convenient communications by land and sea. Thus, soil, aspect, water supply, means of communication, and society combined to make this site desirable about sixteen hundred years ago.

At the outset a few notes on method may be of use to excavators without experience of dealing with such sites.

The excavation of fallen buildings, such as these, is facilitated if the area of fallen masonry is first, after location, cleared of its top soil covering; and then (in dry weather) swept as clean as may be with a stiff besom. This enables the excavator to detect the mortar-bedded flints of wall foundations from random founders of fallen flints and mortar, while up-turn of roofing tiles, nails, and coloured wall-plaster assure him that he is working on fallen material. When a foundation line of mortar-bedded flints has been located, such line should be followed up, outlining it, outside, down to the wall footing, and inside, down to the room floor. Outlining; groping along wall faces; is the right preliminary to the excavation of a building. Such outlining will sometimes be helped in discovery by the occurrence of a narrow vertical slit along the wall face—between it and the fallen masonry—filled with washed grit of split-pea size. I think that this comes from the extra intersticiary soak of surface rain-water, held up by, and soaking off, the hard foundation top surface. Again, sometimes wall flint courses are entirely destroyed by the plough—but the footings of such destroyed walls remain intact below the 4 to 6 inch deep plough disturbance. "Find and follow the footings" is a counsel of perfection for excavators on similar sites—and note, that chalk rubble footings may descend (as here) almost 3 feet below the last course of bedded wall flints—if the subsoil needed such foundation precaution; also note, that the uppermost inches of footings may bulge outwards, *i.e.*, overhang the true outmost vertical line of the wall footing. This appears to have been caused by the pressure of the superimposed weight of wall on the chalk rubble footings at a level where they had the least lateral support, for the chalk rubble of the footings was originally rammed into a trench, of the intended depth and width, dug vertically in the natural soil. According to my experience, Roman wall footings on sound chalk or gravel soil were shallow, whereas, if the subsoil was suspect, sandy and clayey (as here), such footings may be deep.

Then follows the laborious job of wholly clearing out the débris that covers such room floors; this is the only way of getting all the evidence of occupation now obtainable—*cf.* the composite hypocaust in Room 5, and the fireplace in Room 12, and those in the courtyard, none of which would have been recorded if outlining the wall foundations had been held to be adequate excavation. It is not. You must do the sum to prove it. A walled area with floors that yield indications of habitation should be wholly excavated, and proved down to the natural subsoil—if the excavator values a clear conscience. And the débris aforesaid should be dumped outside the outer wall foundations. Always keep a proved floor clear.

When excavation has reached the floor level of occupation, abstain from working on such in wet weather. Puddled chalk floors and mortared surfaces should never be dealt with except in dry weather. "Most haste worst speed." If the excavator continues work on such surfaces when rain falls—or soon after—he is sure to destroy possible evidence by the stabble of his footsteps.

A light prong, of which the tine points should communicate touch and understanding by feel—as do finger-tips; a shovel; and a besom (when in doubt—sweep) are my best tools for such investigation. A plasterer's small trowel, a curved bayonet pick fixed in a handle (devised by Colonel Hawley), and a large blade knife are useful in following a flue. "The spade" is the formular tool that describes Excavation. It is only good for marking out, and for top surface removal work. The spade edge does not communicate *feel.* A light prong is the tool that is the best helper to the enquiring excavator. It communicates feel. It is a real pleasure to feel a difference (and subsequently to prove it) at the buried ends of your prong-tines. A pickaxe is very useful in places where mere removal of débris and soil has got to be done and where there is no fear of destruction; but, like the spade, it only removes, loosens: it is not a tool that feels, and its blow smashes. The use of a pickaxe should be carefully supervised on such sites as this.

The planning of this villa site is deliberate and all of a piece. It does not suggest casual addition, nor revision.

I think, as before said, that this villa was occupied by a well-to-do owner, and that his standard of life was both comfortable and tasteful—judging by the evidence of the building foundations, and of the objects found. He kept warm in winter. He bathed luxuriously. He liked beautiful objects—such as fine glass vessels and Samian pottery. His daily life was secure. No defence was needed against a possible enemy. His land was cultivated, and he kept cattle, horses, sheep, pigs, goats, and dogs. He played games in which bone squares engraved with pips were used. He wrote on wax tablets with iron styli. He wore shoes the soles of which were fortified by iron cleets. His womenfolk plied their needles (but no spindle-whorls were found), and tired their hair with bone hairpins, their arms with bronze and Kimmeridge shale bangles, and their ears with engraved bronze rings, and they used bronze fibulae (safety-pins). Pax Romana ruled in this part of Britain during the period covered by the years A.D. 253–375. We know by casual graffiti on tiles found at Silchester that Latin was written and perhaps spoken there by the native population. We may wonder whether here, thirty-three miles distant, Latin cries to cattle and plough-teams were heard sixteen hundred years ago, along the lowlands beneath the steep slopes of Dean Hill. But whether Latin or Celtic echoes resounded, we may be sure that farm life here was Romanized.

I think that the corridor range of buildings and Bath-house II may have had upper stories, judging by the deep footings of the outer walls, the buttress supports, and by the large amount of fallen débris which covered the site here.

I cannot explain the need for two elaborate, isolated bath-houses to serve the needs of a range of rooms extending 142 feet—except, possibly, by modern experience, *e.g.*, a seventeenth-century house where bath requirements had always been served without a bathroom: on change of occupancy three bathrooms were at once demanded by the new tenant. Luxury, superfluity may have appealed to A.D. 253 as to A.D. 1923. Probably human nature has always endorsed the child's reply who, when asked if his helping of pudding was too much, answered: "I like too much." We do. Perhaps they did. There seems to be a liking of too much in the bath-house provision on this site. *Cf.* Tacitus, "The Life of Cnaeus Julius Agricola," translated by Arthur Murphy, chap. xxi. After praising Agricola's wise regulations (A.D. 80) for educating and Romanizing the Britons, he thus (inconsequently) concludes the chapter: "The consequence was, that they who had always disdained the Roman language, began to cultivate its beauties. The Roman apparel was seen without prejudice, and the toga became a fashionable part of dress. By degrees the charms of vice gained admission to their hearts; baths, and porticoes, and elegant banquets, grew into vogue; and the new manners, which, in fact, served only to sweeten slavery, were, by the unsuspecting Britons called the arts of polished humanity." The "charms of vice" are scarcely suggested by the bath-houses of East Grimstead. Romanized Britain is nearer to our present-day civilization than all the Anglo-Saxon and Mediaeval years intervening. Good Roads, Order, Politic vision, Tolerance, Stability, and Comfort were the foundations on which arose the edifice of Roman rule in the outlying provinces of the Empire—under the protection of the legions guarding the border lands.

The outlying cold Bath-house III of Plans II and VI probably served the needs of slave workers on this farm, of whose habitations there are surface soil indications to the South-East of this bath-house, but excavation has not proved foundations.

I think that Roman villa life ended gradually on this site. Sudden disaster, caused by Saxon invasion, does not seem to have befallen this organized and carefully designed establishment. Evacuation. Desertion. Temporary re-occupation by vagrant squatters. Picking and Stealing. Decay. Roof-timber founders. Renewed Picking and Stealing—all these episodes may have combined to despoil this site of its best materials. Then—sixteen hundred years of dereliction; of ministry of the Seasons; of Worms; and of Agriculture completed the ultimate burial of these buildings, the relics of which I have tried to exhume and record.

EXCAVATIONS AT EAST GRIMSTEAD, WILTSHIRE, 12–14, 17–19, 37–9

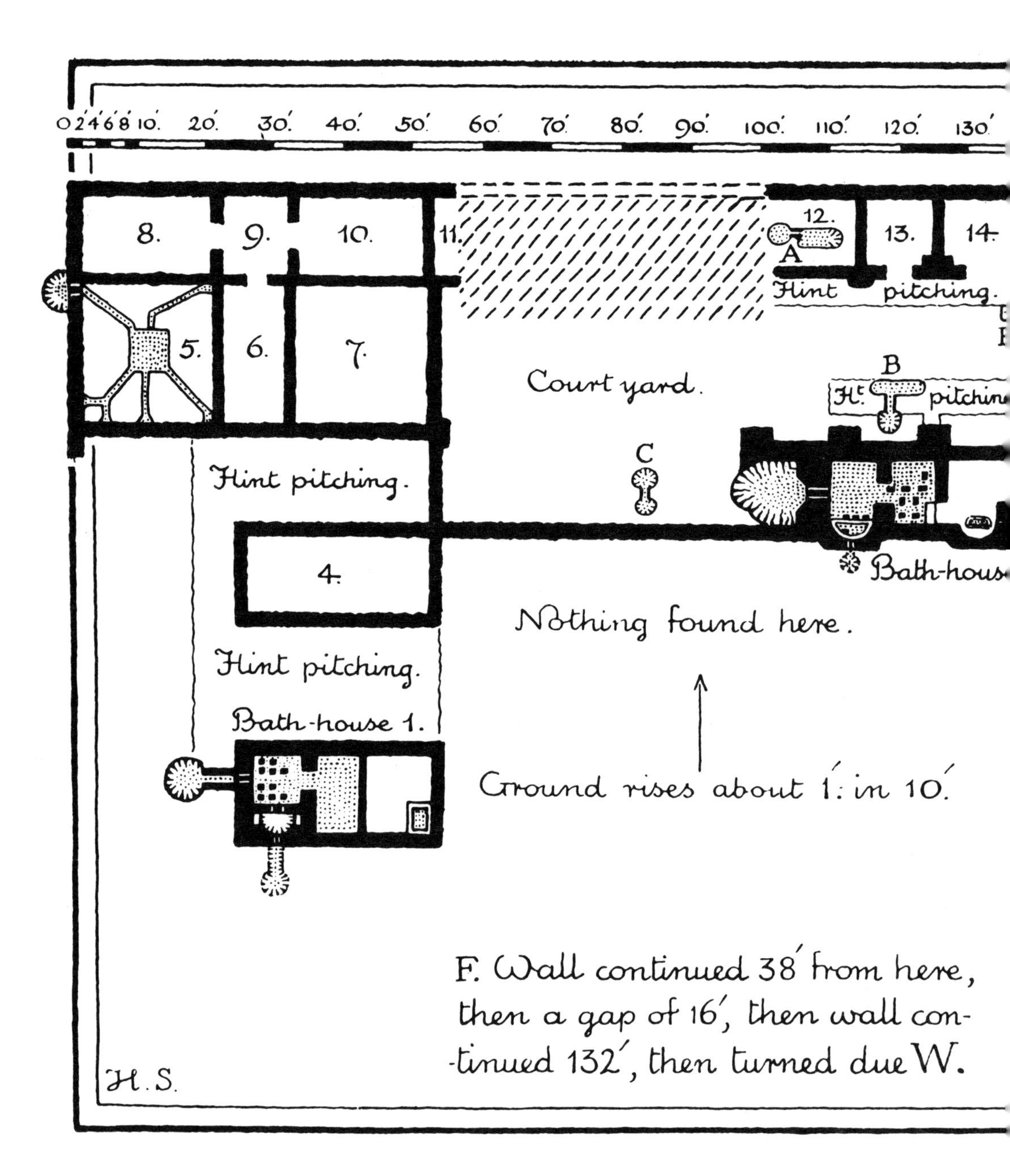
0 2 4 6 8 10. 20. 30. 40. 50. 60. 70. 80. 90. 100. 110. 120. 130.
8.
9.
10.
11.
12.
A
13.
14.
Flint pitching.
5.
6.
7.
Court yard.
B
Ft. pitching
C
Flint pitching.
Bath-house
4.
Nothing found here.
Flint pitching.
Bath-house 1.
Ground rises about 1: in 10.
F. Wall continued 38′ from here, then a gap of 16′, then wall continued 132′, then turned due W.
H.S.

und Plan of Roman Villa Site at

ST GRIMSTEAD WILTS

15.

. Foundations. ▨ = Rained Foundations .
dotted surfaces denote sunken floors. H.S.

. C. Fire places probably made after the evacuation.
Drain running under the wall, roofed with slab stones.
Stone marked with a +. Query_Centurial stone?

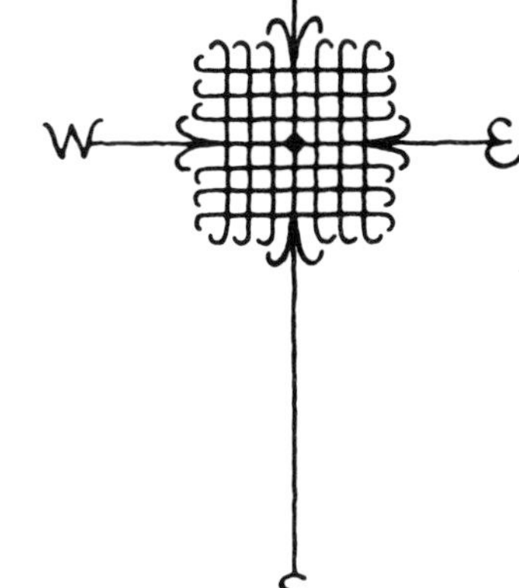

II.

Bath-house 3.

Drain Ditch.

THE ROMAN POTTERY SITE AT ASHLEY RAILS

The place-name of Ashley Rails is distinctive, for "Rails" locally denote the limit between forest and cultivation; *e.g.*, Boldrewood Rails, Burley Rails, Beaulieu Rails; so in this place, a post and rail fence separates Ash-tree meadow from Pitt's Wood.

A name survives owing to curious chances—occupation—an invention—an almanack—a railway time-table—garden plants—such-like different things have prolonged the vanishing life of names. Here, chance commemorates a Surveyor-General of the New Forest in the reign of George III. Foresters may criticize the timber, but Forest lovers will think that John Pitt is fortunate in his memorial. It stands below the hills of Ticketsbury on the South and of Cockley Plain on the North, in a little valley down which meanders Ashley brook on its way to join Ditch-end brook near Green-house Farm. Within the Inclosure tall oaks stretch their twisted, moss-grown limbs above an under-growth of holly bushes and bracken; without, rise heath-clad bluffs crowned with thickets. The site was well chosen; the wood is beautiful; what finer memorial could name desire?

Yet after praise we murmur: John Pitt had no care for archaeology when he set out the limits of his wood in 1775; he only considered tree-planting. The boundary bank and rails of the Inclosure cross an area where Romano-British kilns once burned. The site has been divided and disturbed. The Forester has obstructed the Archaeologist.

Ashley gives its name to the Walk which comprises 4,112 acres at the Northern extremity of the Forest. The site is out of the way, whether the wayfarer follows the high road from Fordingbridge to Southampton, or the track from Frogham to Bramshaw Telegraph and Fritham; it is in a valley hidden from view by level-topped hills, and by Pitt's Wood; accordingly, a plan is given of its surroundings for the guidance of those who may pursue "Itinerarium Curiosum." A plan for the curious—for those who like to see the "Pleäce a Teäle's a-twold o'." The place has its genius, although there is little to see now from an archaeological point of view, but it was the choice of skilful Romanized potters, and it was one of the busy manufacturing centres whence issued the various products of the New Forest Potteries during the latter period of the Roman occupation.

The wayfarer from Fordingbridge should be on the lookout for a field path on the left of the Southampton Road near Avonside. This is a short cut through Sandy Balls to Godshill, and it passes beside a deeply sunken hollow way on the right of the path, called "Scuts Lane," which may have been trampled by the potters' laden ponies on their way to the ford across the Avon at Horse-port. Farther on, a gate across the high road, near "The Fighting Cocks," marks the

Forest boundary. Passing this, the wayfarer stands on a bare ridge from which far views may be obtained to the West, across the Avon, over a distance where Hampshire, Dorset, and Wilts meet, and near views over little valleys channelled by winding brooks flanked by ridges parallel to that of Godshill. The wind-swept expanses of heather are dotted with holly bushes and overgrown with furze, outlying deer may sometimes be seen, and within this century black grouse might have been flushed on the plains. Across this open tract of forest a rough trail leads to the tall trees that fill the Eastern Valley-head, and here is Pitt's Wood, behind which stands Ashley Lodge, with its grounds and browse pens bounded by Ashley Rails.

It is difficult now to imagine manufacturing industry and commercial enterprise in these forest solitudes. But the ancient pottery sites at Ashley Rails, Islands Thorns, Amberwood, and Sloden all lie within a mile radius of the central site at Crock Hill. Such were the ways of life here during the early centuries of our era. In Romano-British times the New Forest Potteries—like the contemporary Castor Potteries—became commercial centres such as had never before arisen in Britain. Pottery requirements were fulfilled far and wide in many sorts of ware. Tastes were studied. Sharp wits were at work noting the products of foreign kilns, and skilled potters were able to imitate Samian, or Gaulish ware, and to meet the demand for such luxuries in the Romanized districts of Britain.

Then, these sites may be said to have been off, rather than out of the way. A mile distant to the North ran the ridge way which was called "the herepath" in Saxon boundaries of Downton and which we may suppose was a way long before the Saxon invaders used it.

Three miles distant to the West was Horse-port on the Avon—now a suburb of Fordingbridge—where water-borne traffic may have come and gone, up and down the river. Farther West, nine miles distant, ran Achling Dyke, the Roman road from Sorbiodunum (Old Sarum) to Durnovaria (Dorchester), with a branch at Badbury Rings leading to Morionio (Hamworthy).

The white clay of Lytchett near Hamworthy, the grey clay of Holwell near Cranbourne, and the yellow clay of Verwood would all have been within easy reach if wanted to supplement the near-by forest clays; while the blue gault clay of the Isle of Wight—to which Mr. Thomas May ascribes the hard "thumb-pot" ware—may have been brought *via* Lepe or Lymington. As to fuel, these potters had not far to seek. All the evidence points to forest conditions having existed in this district from time immemorial. Thus we may regard these sites as having been well adapted to their purpose. When the Roman era came to an end in the fifth century, and when the Saxon invaded this part of Britain, the New Forest Potteries shared in the common disaster. The industry perished with the

ROMAN POTTERY SITE
ASHLEY RAILS NEW FOREST.
I
II
3.
4.
4.
5.
H.S.
I. & II. Kiln Sites. 3. Mound with mortar floor.
4. 4. Mortar floor, which continues beneath 5.
S
E W
N

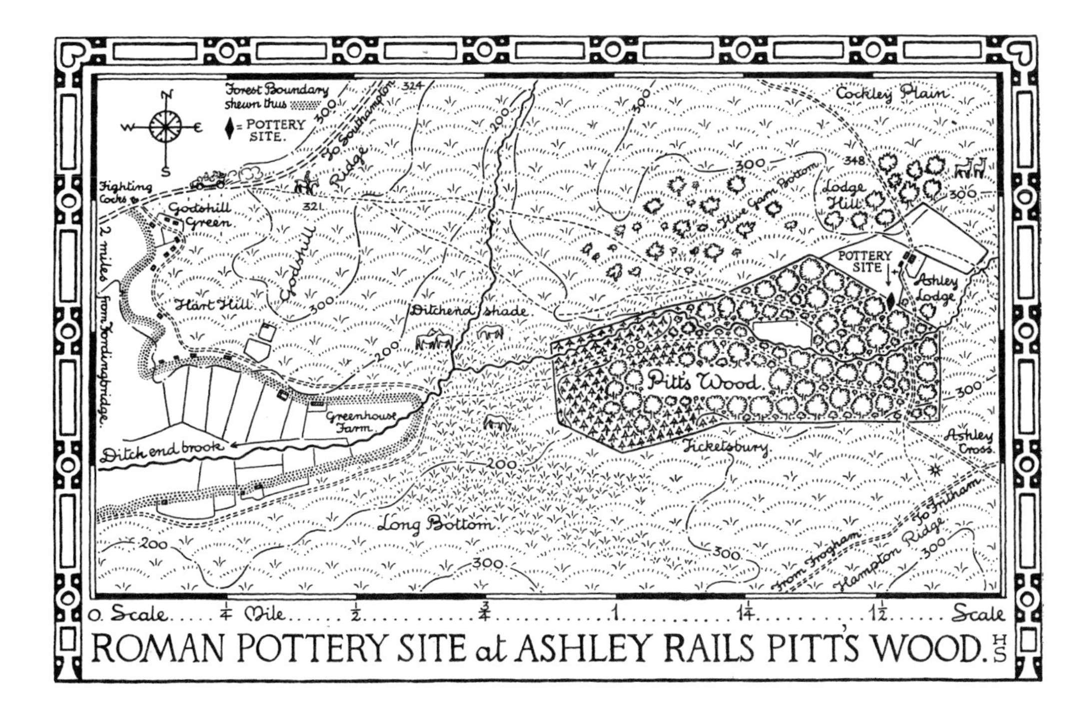

ROMAN POTTERY SITE at ASHLEY RAILS PITT'S WOOD. H S

civilization which it served. The potter's wheel came to a dead halt. Commerce was set back for centuries, and these manufacturing sites became derelict, and finally sank into oblivion, which has deepened during the lapse of fifteen centuries.

A Crown keeper's ill luck with his pony, and its burial in a field near the rails of Pitt's Wood, brought instead good luck to me. Chance often favours archaeological discovery. There were no signs of humps or hollows in the field surface, nor had tell-tale sherds been turned up by the plough, but the keeper's hole-digging of final purpose revealed a thick layer of ashes and sherds about three feet below the top surface. From this description it seemed likely that the pottery site on the Pitt's Wood side of the rails might extend into the field.

Here was an opportunity. All the other New Forest Pottery sites are overgrown with trees, and impossible to excavate. This corner of the field was possible, and I have to thank G. H. Slightam, the Crown keeper, for his information, and for the facilities which he was always ready to give in order to help my subsequent excavation.

I began with the hope of finding a kiln site that could be planned, for the previous records of excavations in New Forest Pottery sites by Bartlett and by Wise lack such information. This hope was not fulfilled. My experience was

1.
2.
3.
4.
5.
6.
7.
8.
9.
10.
11.
H.S.

similar to theirs. Brick-like lumps, burnt sandstone and slag refuse, were found in defined circular patches, but the kilns were broken down. Nothing stood that could be measured and figured as a typical New Forest kiln plan. Only scattered building material remained. Good luck befell otherwise, namely, in the discovery of some distinctive pottery, *i.e.*, stamped ware, which had not then been identified as of British manufacture in published records.

The times compelled intermittent and single-handed excavation. From December 1917 to October 1918, I averaged five days a month digging at Ashley Rails, and though progress was slow, the excavation gained thereby in sureness, when the kiln levels were reached, and when every upturned spit yielded ash-clogged sherds for estimation—either to be kept as specimens of ware, or to be again cast away.

EXCAVATIONS IN NEW FOREST ROMAN POTTERY SITES, 11–14

OLD SLODEN WOOD

The excavations made by J. P. Bartlett and J. R. Wise (*circa* 1860) at Crock Hill and Islands Thorns do not leave much hope for further discoveries on these sites. Notwithstanding, in order to make sure, I dug a trial trench in 1919 for 20 feet, followed by trial holes for another 20 feet, through the apparently least disturbed area of Crock Hill pottery site. But in vain; throughout the length of the trench, and in all the holes, there were signs of previous excavation; so I gave up hoping to find an undisturbed kiln here.

Investigations at Islands Thorns led me to the same conclusion. The only knowledge now obtainable on these sites is from sherds showing the different wares which the Romanized potters made there.

There remained Sloden and Black Heath Meadow (where J. P. Bartlett records no excavation and J. R. Wise but little) as the last chance of finding an undisturbed New Forest Pottery Kiln; and chance, as at Ashley Rails, provided the opportunity for discovery. I am indebted to a Fritham woodman, Parnell by name, who told me of a site in Old Sloden Wood, near Sloden Green, where rabbits threw up black earth and sherds on their scrapes—it was neither overgrown by trees, nor showed surface signs of previous disturbance, so discovery seemed possible, though the indications aforesaid were much less both in area and quantity than on other New Forest Pottery sites.

The wooded ridge of Sloden Hill is a landmark from afar if it is approached from the West. The wayfarer who crosses Ibsley Common, Ogdens Purlieu, and

ROMANIZED POTTERS OF
SLODEN & THEIR WARES
H.S

Hasley Hills, has traversed open heaths and sandy knolls for a distance of four miles before he reaches his goal. Then a steep "white-shoot" winds up the hill, the scene changes, and the shadowy woodland of Old Sloden begins. Old yews, white-beams, oaks, and hollies crown the narrow ridge along which the track meanders, visions of blue distance fill gaps between the trees on either side, stubble of past fern-harvest covers the glades, gradually the ridge widens and becomes a hill-top plateau at Sloden Green. Here is our site. It lies 150 paces East from Sloden Green gate, surrounded by a grove of old oaks, yews, hollies, and thorns, up which ivy trees with stems like hawsers climb as best they can, spreading into criss-cross branching as they seek for a place in the sun.

"Trees be company," so William Barnes divined, and so I found while excavating here, alone, throughout February 1920. Their presence is felt, near, but aloof, and their sounds are heard as the wind sways their branches to and fro—aerial sounds of rubbing, creaking, and snapping. Besides this company, deer, ponies, cattle, rabbits, squirrels, owls, and wood-peckers were my companions. Deer are inquisitive. They stand at gaze—then bound away—then stop to gaze once more, before finally deciding to avoid the intruder. Ponies ignore intrusion, they are bent on feed; not so cattle, their curiosity is tiresome. Rabbits and squirrels seem to want to know, but fear knowledge. Owls hoot to each other all day long, wood-peckers yaffle to themselves. Such was my estimate of company in Old Sloden Wood.

Excavation here soon showed that a pit of some kind lay below ground. The filling consisted of black earth interspersed with burnt stuff and sherds. Eventually a stoke-hole was uncovered, surrounded on three sides by ramps dug out of the natural plateau gravel subsoil, and bounded on the fourth side by a wall of yellow puddled clay which crossed the stoke-hole. The top surface of this clay wall was then followed and uncovered. Excavation proved that it changed in colour from yellow to red towards the centre, and was surrounded, flush, by the natural gravel subsoil floor. The centre of this top red clay surface was then searched for indication of an oven—which was found—then the vertical face of the stoke-hole yellow clay wall was searched for indication of a flue entrance—which also was found—after which the excavation proceeded according to plan.

In the stoke-hole large sherds were found on the gravel ramps on either side of the flue entrance, elsewhere they were of smaller size, and not in abundance. There was no large accumulation of black burnt earth and few pieces of charcoal (oak). The floor was gravel subsoil.

In the Flue nothing was found except burnt stuff and fallen lumps of clay burnt grey-black, but at the stoke-hole entrance the bottom half of a coarse ware bowl was bedded, inverted, in the flue floor, to reinforce it at this place of special wear

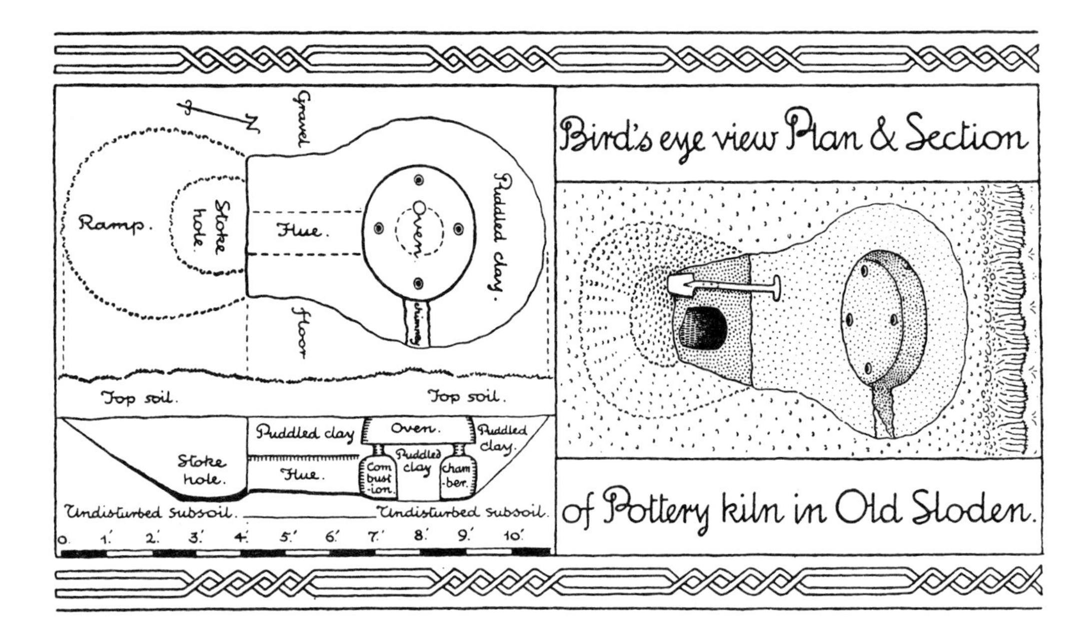

and tear. The fall in the run of the flue floor towards the combustion chamber may be accidental; this part of the floor was in a decayed condition.

In the Combustion Chamber the filling was found to consist of a confused jumble of lumps of clay burnt grey-black and red, sherds, burnt stuff, and charcoal. When the excavation had got down about one foot below the top puddled clay surface, a difference was shown in the filling of the sides and of the centre. The sides were filled with burnt stuff, many lumps and slabs of clay burnt grey-black, some of which showed remains of circular vent-holes, about 1.05 inches diameter, charcoal, and many large sherds, of which some belonged to distorted and over-burnt "wasters." The centre was filled with a core of clay burnt red, interspersed with thin layers of ash. A spell of dry weather enabled me to appreciate the difference in material between the centre and the sides without confusing my up-turn by treading it into mud. After much puzzling over the evidence supplied by the ruinous filling described above, I came to the conclusion that the central core of clay burnt red represents the remains of a solid puddled clay column of which the top formed part of the oven floor, that the thin layers of ash represent cracks that had been filled in with burnt ash by the fiery draught of the furnace, that the slabs of clay burnt grey-black, some of which showed vent-holes represent a fallen vent-holed floor that extended from the top of the column

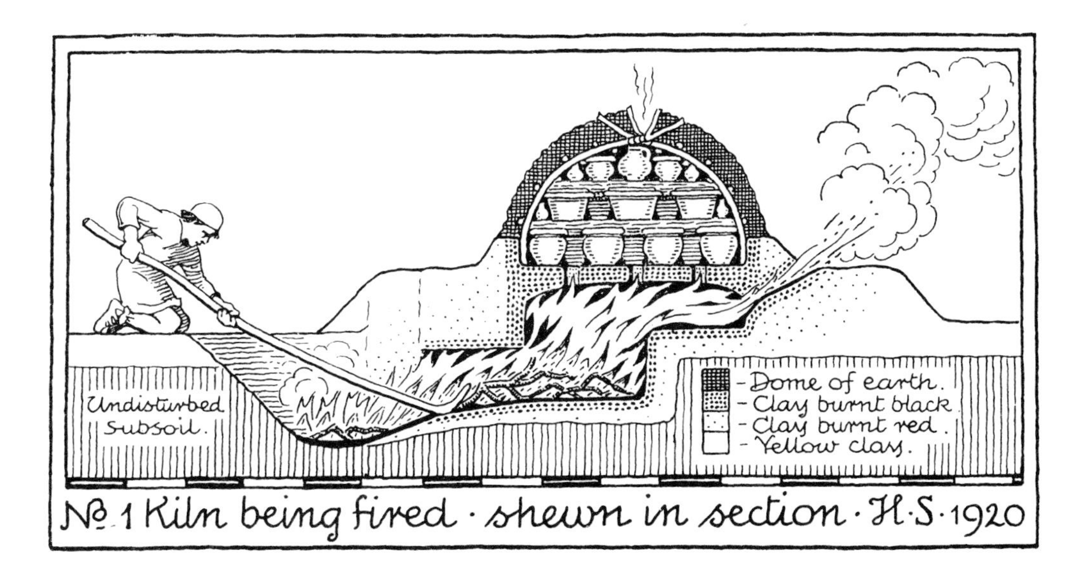

No 1 Kiln being fired · shewn in section · H·S·1920

to the sides, thus completing the oven floor, and that the lumps of similar material represent the foundered side-wall lining of the combustion chamber that was exposed to the direct flames of the furnace. In several instances these lumps showed a roughly smoothed surface.

The position of the chimney is different from that of the chimneys in Kilns I and II, Sloden Inclosure, and of the kilns at Linwood. I suppose because the central clay column supporting the vent-holed oven floor would have obstructed a direct through draught.

The ground adjoining was then searched by means of trial trenches and hole-digging, with the result that evidence of black earth and scattered sherds was found only on the North side for a distance of ten yards; this kiln was not surrounded by a puddled clay floor, as were the kilns in Sloden Inclosure near by.

In the course of this search through the adjacent woodland, a wasted earthwork was discovered, which had hitherto been overlooked. It is most clearly defined on the South-Eastern side of this kiln site, and inside Sloden Inclosure. At both these places it appears as a broad, low, gravelly bank, about 12 paces wide, about 2 feet high, and with indications of a silted up ditch on the outside. Elsewhere, it appears as a slight rise and fall of the woodland floor—but its continuity is unmistakable. This wasted earthwork encloses an oval area, 170 paces by 120 paces, on the South-Eastern side of which is the kiln described above, and on the Western another kiln site which, judging by the quantity of black earth and sherds upturned by the rabbits, was much longer in use. Unfortunately it is now overgrown with trees which obstruct excavation. Owing to modern trackways and the waste of time, no original entrance can be located. The breadth and consolidation of the bank described indicate antiquity, while the position of these kiln sites, within the circling earthwork, point to their connection. This earthwork appears to have enclosed a sort of krall for the potters' convenience—either to keep in stock or to keep out wolves—perhaps for both purposes. None of the existing earthworks connected with New Forest Pottery sites indicates defence against hostile neighbours' raids. The Romano-British potters worked in peace, and in plenty—so far as clay and fuel were concerned; but I failed to locate with certainty a habitation site here. Yet perhaps this high and dry krall, with springs issuing on the adjacent hill-side, may have served such purpose. They appear to have been poor folk. Certainly they dropped few coins, and no bronze ornaments. They may have been content to live, as gypsies live nowadays, in bee-hive tents amid the shelter of forest thickets, which living would leave small trace behind it after the lapse of eighteen centuries.

EXCAVATIONS IN NEW FOREST ROMAN POTTERY SITES, 49–54

A POTTER'S HUT NEAR ISLANDS THORNS

For a long time past I have sought to discover a dwelling connected with one of the New Forest Roman pottery sites, and have played the earthwork game of hide-and-seek in vain—up to now—when at length *seek* has defeated *hide*.

The difficulty in this instance was that such dwellings were presumably of slight construction, and so their ground plans would have been destroyed either by tree-planting, drain-cutting, or cultivation. The pottery sites at Sloden, Amberwood, Crock Hill, and Islands Thorns are now in the midst of tree-planted, drained inclosures; at Pitt's Wood and Ashley Rails—half tree-planted, half under cultivation; at Linwood—wholly under cultivation; and accordingly all the above sites had been searched in vain for habitation evidence. In 1925, however, good chance led me to examine the plain outside Islands Thorns Inclosure (300 yards distant N.W. from the pottery site) where, South of the Ordnance Survey bench mark 367 feet above the sea, there is a high spring outflow from the plateau gravel. This spring, and the adjoining dry gravel subsoil, suggested attractions for possible habitation; and so they proved to have been; for here, on a grassy plat of undisturbed Forest land, sheltered by self-sown oaks, thorns, and hollies, an ovalish depression was found, surrounded by a slight, irregular bank, 25 feet over-all from East to West, 20 feet over-all from

North to South. The irregular bank rising about 1 foot 3 inches above the central depression, and from 6 inches to 9 inches above the surrounding ground. The depression measured about 10 feet from East to West, and 7 feet from North to South. Irregularity was a feature of this slight earthwork.

About 10 yards distant to the West rabbits worked in the soil and threw up Roman pottery in their scrapes. Scattered near by there were five shallow, roundish depressions in the ground surface, about 10 feet to 12 feet in diameter, and 1 foot deep. The whole site suggested discovery, and was one that could be excavated, for the self-sown trees had been most obliging in their sowing, and did not interfere with possible excavation.

In March 1925 I again obtained the help of Walter Brown, and we were lucky in having a dry spell of weather throughout the period (eight days) of excavation and filling-in here.

We began by uncovering the ovalish depression surrounded by an irregular bank. A consolidated, trodden clay floor was found lying 9 inches below the depression top surface, and 1 foot 3 inches as our excavation advanced below the surrounding irregular bank, which was not consolidated like the floor, but appeared to be formed of loose rubble clay lying on trodden clay, a floor of two levels. Excavation of the whole area revealed six post-holes in the pentagonal position shown in the plan, which gave the floor size of the hut, namely, about 15 feet 6 inches in length by 11 feet in width. The holes varied from 9 inches by 8 inches in diameter, 9 inches deep, to 6 inches by 5 inches diameter, 8 inches deep; fragments of black decayed wood adhered to their sides and bottoms, and they were filled with soil in which bracken roots descended. Such growth helped to locate these holes—after the excavated clay floor had been swept quite clean with a besom. We were also helped by a spell of fine weather, as the hole-fillings dried out a different colour from that of the adjoining trodden clay floor.

The curious position of the post-holes on the North-west and West sides of the hut that make a pentagon ground plan, suggest precaution for wind resistance on these sides where certainly wind now blows most fiercely across the plain. I am told that in Canada such zigzag method of fencing (with purpose of staying the direct wind blast impact on a length of stockade) is now used, and is called a "snake-fence."

I suppose the hut floor to have been spanned by lean-to principals fixed in these holes, and tied together, atop, by a ridge pole, with sidings of wattle-work (at which the potters were expert) covered by skins as a roof, and with a ramp of clay piled all round the outside base of the wattle-work in order to deflect rain-water falling on the roof from soaking on to the hut floor, and also to give warmth and support. When the hut was abandoned, and as its lean-to principals gradually

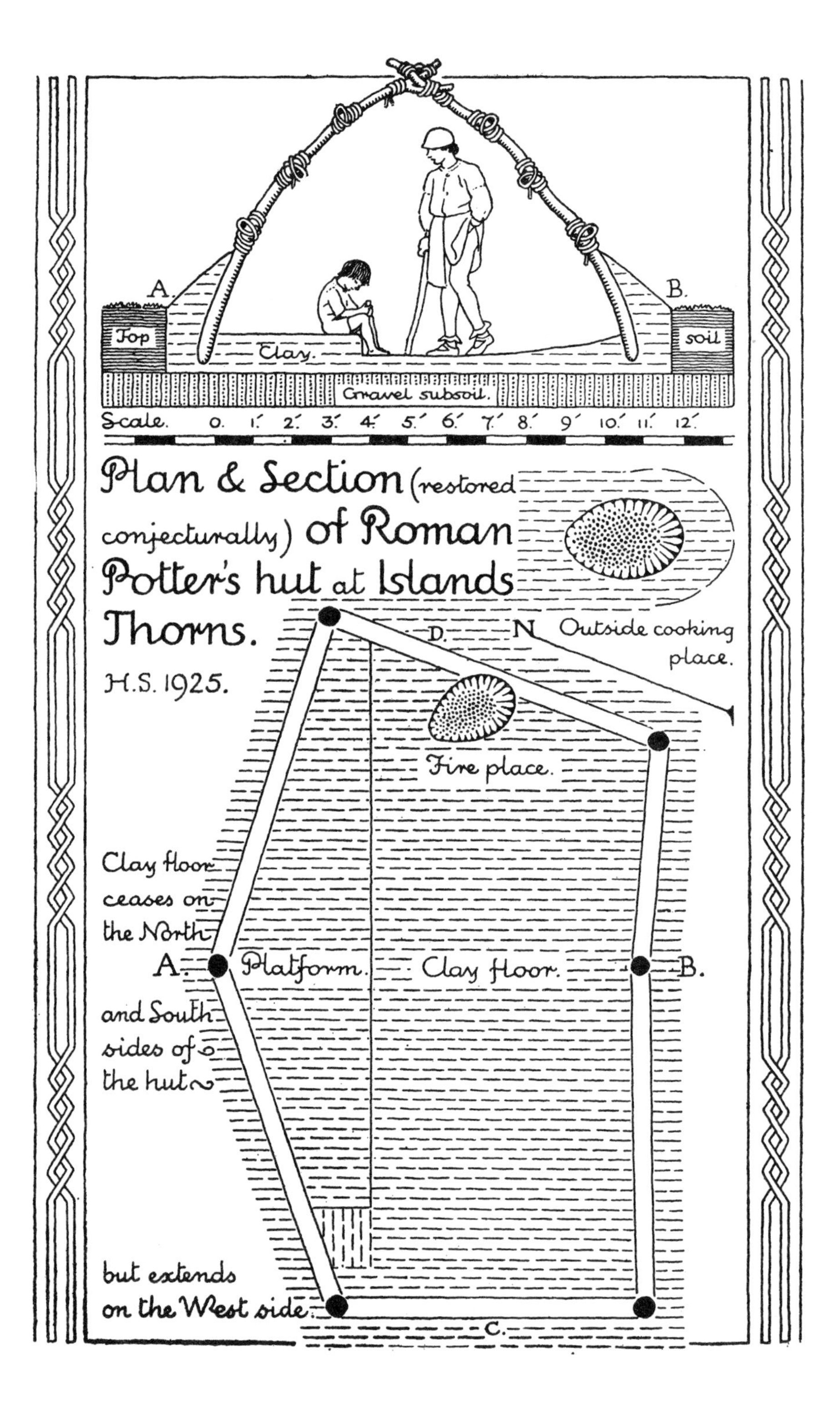
A.
B.
Top
soil
Clay.
Gravel subsoil.
Scale. 0. 1.' 2.' 3.' 4.' 5.' 6.' 7.' 8.' 9.' 10.' 11.' 12.'
Plan & Section (restored conjecturally) of Roman Potter's hut at Islands Thorns.
H.S. 1925.
D.
N
Outside cooking place.
Fire place.
Clay floor ceases on the North
A.
Platform.
Clay floor.
B.
and South sides of the hut
but extends on the West side.
C.

decayed, such surrounding clay ramp would have subsided unevenly, and eventually formed the irregular bank which encircled the depression as seen before excavation.

The difference in the floor levels mentioned above was caused by the Northern side being raised 6 inches above the Southern side (see section). This raised level was 3 feet 9 inches wide from post-hole A (see plan) to the edge of the platform, and extended to the Eastern side of the hut, but ended 2 feet 6 inches from the Western side in a clay ramp. I suppose that this platform was used as a sleeping place; if so, the Eastern end of the platform, near the fireplace, must have been crowded in cold weather. I imagine potters at the end of their day's work squatting on this platform before a glowing inside fireplace, warming their hands, stiff and swollen with cold manipulation of wet clay into vessel forms; and then, when warmed, and tired of talk, sleeping on the dry, fern-bedded platform, with children cuddling toy pottery beside dying embers of the fire below, in security. For no outside defences were needed. No enemy feared. Pax Romana seems to have ruled here all through the period when this industry flourished.

EXCAVATIONS IN NEW FOREST ROMAN POTTERY SITES, 101–4

HEYWOOD SUMNER: His Archaeological and Topographical Bibliography

The bibliography offered here is complete as far as is known. In the first part Sumner's own books are listed while in the second there appear major works to which he has contributed topographical or archaeological illustrations. But no attempt has been made to include the numerous other volumes, principally children's stories, enlivened by his illustrations.

The abbreviations used are:

BNSSP	*Bournemouth Natural Science Society's Proceedings*
PDNHAFC	*Proceedings of the Dorset Natural History and Archaeological Field Club*
PHFCAS	*Proceedings of the Hampshire Field Club and Archaeological Society*

1881 *The Itchen Valley from Tichbourne to Southampton* (Seeley, Jackson & Halliday: London).

1882 *The Avon from Naseby to Tewkesbury* (Seeley, Jackson & Halliday: London).

1888 *The Besom-Maker and other Country-Folk Songs* (Longmans: London).

1910 *The Book of Gorley* (Chiswick Press: London).

1913 *The Ancient Earthworks of Cranborne Chase* (Chiswick Press: London).

1913 'The Ancient Earthworks of Cranborne Chase.' *PDNHAFC* XXXIV (1913), 31–41.

1914 *Excavations on Rockbourne Down, Hampshire* (Chiswick Press: London).

1916 'Excavation on a Roman Villa site near East Grimstead.' In F. Stevens (ed.), *The Festival Book of Salisbury*, 14–23.

1917 *The Ancient Earthworks of the New Forest* (Chiswick Press: London).

1919 *A Descriptive Account of the Roman Pottery made at Ashley Rails, New Forest* (Chiswick Press: London).

1920 'Old Maps of Hampshire, Dorset and Wiltshire.' *BNSSP* XI (1918–19), 52–5.

1921 'Ancient Earthworks in the Bournemouth District.' *BNSSP* XII (1919–20), 48–67 (= *Local Papers*, 11–39).

1921 *A Descriptive Account of the Roman Pottery Sites at Sloden and Blackheath Meadow, Linwood, New Forest* (Chiswick Press: London).

1923 *A Map of ancient sites in the New Forest, Cranborne Chase and Bournemouth district* (Bournemouth).

1923 'Excavations of Barrows on Ibsley Common.' *BNSSP* XIV (1921–2), 68–78 (= *Local Papers*, 107–20).

1924 *A Guide to the New Forest* (Brown & Son: Ringwood).

1924 *Excavations at East Grimstead, Wiltshire* (Chiswick Press: London).

1925 'An Account of Alresford by Sir G. B. Rodney.' *PHFCAS* IX, 334–41.

1925 'A Winter Walk in the New Forest.' PHFCAS IX, 361–9 (= *Local Papers*, 179–194).

1926 'New Forest and Old Woods.' *BNSSP* XVIII (1925–6), 48–58.

1927 *Excavations in New Forest Roman Pottery Sites* (Chiswick Press: London).

1927 'Excavation of a (Roman) pottery kiln at Rough-Piece, Linwood.' *PHFCAS* X, 81–2.

1927 'Archaeological Benefactors. Hampshire, Dorset and Wiltshire.' *BNSSP* XIX (1926–7), 61–87 (= *Local Papers*, 49–86).

1927 'Note on a bronze hoard in the New Forest.' *Antiq. Journ.* VII, 192.

1929 'Natural landmarks in Bournemouth and New Forest Districts.' *BNSSP* XXI (1928–9), 84–91 (= *Local Papers*, 121–32).

1929 'J. Nörden's Survey of Medieval coppice in the New Forest AD 1609.' *PHFCAS* X, 95–117 (= *Local Papers*, 147–78).

1930 'Coombs Ditch and Bokerly Dyke reviewed.' *BNSSP* XXII (1929–30), 99–112 (= *Local Papers*, 87–106).

1930 'Mammoth Tusk Discovery at Ibsley.' *PDNHAFC* 52, 59–74 (= *Local Papers*, 133–46).

1931 *Local Papers, Archaeological and Topographical. Hampshire, Dorset and Wiltshire* (Chiswick Press: London).

1931 'Earthwork at "The Nodes" Beaulieu Heath.' *PHFCAS* X, 293.

1933 'Survey of Moorlands near Verwood.' *PDNHAFC* 54, 233–56.

1934 'Cranborne Chase.' In S. Watson Smith, *The Book of Bournemouth*, 129–44 (Bournemouth).

1934 'New Forest.' In S. Watson Smith, *The Book of Bournemouth*, 158–74 (Bournemouth).

1883 J. R. Wise, *The New Forest* (Southerans Artists Edition).

1884 E. N. Buxton, *Epping Forest* (Edward Stanford: London).

1922 W. G. Wallace, 'Excavations on St. Catherine's Hill, Christchurch.' BNSSP XIII (1920–1), 63–6.

1924 F. Stevens, *Stonehenge Today and Yesterday* (HMSO: London).

GENERAL BIBLIOGRAPHY

Fulford, M. G. 1975: *New Forest Roman Pottery: manufacture and distribution with a corpus of the pottery types* (Oxford, BAR 17).

Groube, L. M. and Bowden, M. C. B. 1982: *The Archaeology of Rural Dorset* (Monograph No. 4 of the Dorset Natural Hist. & Archaeol. Soc.).

Hawkins, D. 1980: *Cranborne Chase* (London).

Pasmore, A. 1967: *New Forest Pottery Kilns and Earthworks* (Cadenham).

Royal Commission on Historical Monuments (England) 1970–75: *Dorset* Vols II-V (HMSO).

Shennan, S. J. and Schadla Hall, R. T. (eds.) 1981: *The Archaeology of Hampshire* (Monograph No. 1 of the Hants. Field Club & Archaeol. Soc.).

Tubbs, C. R. 1968: *The New Forest: an Ecological History* (Newton Abbot).

Williams-Freeman, J. P. 1915: *An Introduction to Field Archaeology as illustrated by Hampshire* (London).

INDEX

Numerals in **bold** type refer to Introductions by Barry Cunliffe

Abbeycroft Down 83
Abbotswood 130
Achling Dyke 83, 137
Akercombe Bottom 62
Alresford Pond 20
Amberwood 100, 101, 137, 146
Ambrosius, Aurelianus (British leader) 46
Ampress 96, 98
Andover 130
Anglo-Saxons 89
animals
 badgers 38
 cattle 40, 64, 104, 110, 127, 132, 143
 cows 40
 deer 38, 43, 44, 55, 64–5, 66, 110, 125, 127, 143
 dogs 22, 23, 127, 132
 foxes 38
 goats 132
 horses 22–3, 127, 132
 hares 23
 lizards 39
 moles 69–70
 pigs/swine 63, 64, 104, 127, 132
 ponies 40–3, 64, 143
 rabbits 38, 143
 sheep 22, 127, 132
 snakes 39
 squirrels 143
 stoats 38
 weasels 38
Anses (earthwork) 104–06
 Wood 25, 44
apples 58–61
Appleslade Inclosure 24, 25, 62, 65
Art Nouveau **10**, **11**
Arts and Crafts movement **9**, **10**, **18**
Art Workers Guild **10**
Ashley Cross 100
Ashley Rails 100, **118**, 136–41, 146
Ashmore 77, 125
Avebury 89
Avon river/valley **11**, 20, 27, 31, 35, 38, 40, 46, 70, **73**, 85, 98, 112, 114, 119, 125, 136, 137

Badbury Rings 40, 83–5, 128, 137
Barnes, William 143
barrows 30, 33, 107, 109, **118**, **119**, 121, 123
 disk 87, 107, 121, 124
Beardsley, Aubrey **10**
bee-gardens 95, 104
Benson, W. A. S. **9**, **10**
birds
 curlews 38
 jays 110
 kingfishers 38
 larks 23
 nightjars 38, 39
 owls 110, 143
 partridges 38
 pheasants 38
 plovers 23
 rooks 27
 snipe 38
 stone curlews 23
 wild duck 38
 woodpeckers 110, 143
Black Heath Meadow **118**, 141
Blackmore Vale 85
Blandford Forum 85
Blandford Race-down 80, 86
Bokerley Dyke 86
Boldrewood 56
bone finds 127

Bossington 130
Bourne (stream) 20
Bournemouth **11**, **18**, 57
  Natural History Society **12**, **74**
bracken/fern 30–1, 44, 46
Bramdean 20
Bramshaw Telegraph 125, 136
Bratley 64
Bratley Plain 98, 100
Breamore Down Mizmaze 89–92
Bride (stream) 22
Bridehead 20
British tribal camps 81, 85, 87
Broadwood, John (folk-song collector) **17**
Brogenslade 33, 38, 51, 54
Broomy 40, 66
Broomy Inclosure 65
Broomy Lodge 65
Browning, Robert 75
Bronze Age **12**, 100
Buckland Rings 95–8
Buddles 55
Bulbarrow 44
Burley 112
Bushy Bratley 25, 27
Buxbury Hill 81
Buzbury Rings 80, 85–6

Cadbury 85
Cadenham (Cadnam) 40
Camden, William, his *Britannia* (1789) 83
Castle Ditches 81–3
Castle Hill 46
Castle Piece, Roe Wood 64, 65, 98–100
caterpillars 30
Celtic burials 33
Century Guild **10**
Cerdic (West Saxon king) 46
chalk soil 19, 20
Charford, battle of 85
Chettle Down 80
Chilbolton 130
Chiselbury 83
Christchurch 98
cider **18**, 51
  cider making 58–61
circles, earth/stone 87, 89
Cockley Plain 136
coins 127
Commoners 50, 54–5
cooking stones 127
Cranborne Chase 40, **73**, 75, 85, 87, 89, 107, 117, 127
  bones preserved on 64
  earthworks **73**, 75–9, 100
Crane, Walter 10
Crawford, O. G. S. (archaeologist) **74**
cremation 107, 123
Crock Hill(s) 100, 101, **118**, 127, 137, 141, 146
Crow 112
Cuckoo Hill **11**, **12**, **18**, 24, 38, 50, 52, 53, 65, 70, **74**, 75, 119

Damerham Knoll 125
Day, Lewis **11**
Dean Brook 117, 129, 130
Dean Hill 129, 132
dew ponds 19
Dibden 113
Digden bog 62
Digden Bottom 65
Dissenters 56–7
Docken's Water 25, 35, 62, 65, 104, 119
Domesday Book 104, 112, 113, 114
Dorchester 20, 79, 83, 128, 137
Dorridge 33, 50, 51, 52
Down Barn 124
Downton 40, 49, 100, 137
Druids 87
Dudsbury 74, **119**

earthworks 62–4, **73–4**, 75–113, 131, 124, 125
  New Forest 92–5
  see also individual place-names
East Grimstead **117**, **118**, 129, 130, 133
Eling 113
Ellingham 27
Emery Down 56
excavation, limitations of human 69–70
  notes on method 130–2

Eyeworth 35, 102
Eyeworth Wood 66

field archaeology 12, 93–5, 101
Figsbury Ring 89
First World War 12, 26, 117, 118
Fitzroy Picture Society **10**
Ford, Roman road at 77
Fordingbridge 35, 40, 100, 136, 137
Forest, The *see* New Forest
forestry for supply and profit 25
Frankenbury 96
Fritham 31, 40, 66, 119, 136
Frogham 40, 136
Frome, river 20
Furze Hill 44, 50, 51, 53

Gallows Hill 86
Gilpin, William, his *Remarks on Forest Scenery* (1794) 63, 95
glow-worms 38
Godshill 40, 52, 136, 137
Gorley **11**, 44, 50, 51, 52, 54, 55, 104, **118**
Great Chibden Gutter 34
Great Chibden Bottom 38, 53, 54, 55, 65
Great Yews 125
Greenford Bottom 62, 64, 65, 98
Grims Ditch **73**, 86
Grimstead Beeches 129
Gussage Down 80, 86

Hambledon Hill 79–81, 83, 85
Hampshire Field Club and Archaeological Society **12**
Hamworthy 79, 83, 128, 137
Handycross 40
Hanford 79
Harbridge 27
Harbridge Church 26
Hasley 31, 68
Hasley Hills 143
Hasley Inclosure 68, 70
heath fires 18, 31, 50–6, 67
heather 31, 34, 40, 46, 56
Hengistbury Head **117**
Hereford Cathedral map 89

Highwood 40
Highwood Farm 40
Hiscock's Hill 31
Hod Hill 80, 83, 85
Holbury 130
Holly Hatch 64
Holly Hatch and Anses Wood 43
Holt Forest 78
Holwell 137
Hordle 113
Horne, Herbert **10**
Hucklesbrook 35, 38, 51, 119
hunting 23, 43, 44
Hurstbourne 20
Hurstbourne Priors 130
Hurstbourne Tarrant 20
Hutchins, Rev. John, his *History of Dorset* 89

Ibsley 27
  church 27
  Common 30, 32, 33, 34, 50, 51, 54, 55, 62, 65, 68–9, 70, **118**, **119**, 119, 121, 141
  House 27
  Park 27, **119**
  street 27
Islands Thorns 100, 101, **118**, 129, 137, 141, 146
Island's Thorn and Amberwood Wood 43
Isle of Wight 40, 113, 137
Itchen, river 20

Julius Caesar 87
Jutish invaders 98

Keyhaven Marshes 112–14
Kimmeridge shale bangles 132
Knap Hill Camp 80, 83
Knighton Wood 125
Knoll Down 86
Knowlton 87–9

labyrinths 89–92
Ladywell 34, 51
Langton Long 86

Latchmoor 40, 50
Latchmore Brook 102
Leadenhall 38, 55, 65
Linford 62
Linwood 34
  kiln excavation at **119**, 145, 146
Linwood bog 34, 35, 38, 52, 55
Little Chibden Bottom 65
London **9**, **11**, 44
Longcross 40
Longstock 130
Longworth **10**
Lymington 98, 113, 114, 137
Lymington, river 96, 98
Lyndhurst 114
  annual show of New Forest ponies 43
Lyndhurst, Manor of 114
Lytchett, near Hamworthy 137

Mackmurdo, Arthur **10**
mammoth tusk, excavation of **119**
Mark Ash Wood 27, 109
Martin Wood 125
mazes *see* labyrinths
Middle Chase Farm 86
Milkham Inclosure 64, 65, 98
Milkham Wood 43
Minstead 56
Mistleberry Wood 100
Mockbeggar 31, 51, 62, 119
Mons Badonicus, battle of 85
Morris, William **9**, **10**

Nadder Valley 81
New Farm 125
New Forest **11**, **12**, **17**, **18**, 24, 26, 27, 31, 32, 39–49, 55, 61–70, 78, **118**, 129, 130
  boundary 32
  cattle 40, 64
  disc barrows 107
  earthworks **74**, 92–5, 104
  laws 43
  pottery 100, 101, 104, **118**, 136–49
  rights 33, 41
  Verderer's Court 43
  'Winter Walk in' **19**, 61–70
  see also trees

Newlands 50
Newland's Bridge 38, 65
Newtown 33, 53
Norden, John 25
North End 27
North Hollow gravel-pit 53
nuncheon time 23
Nursling 130

Oakley Down 89, 107
Ocknell 40
Ocknell Plain 56, 104
Ogdens Purlieu 62, 68, 70, 141
Old Alresford **18**
Old Sarum 77, 83, 125, 128, 130, 137
Old Sloden 27, 64, 67
Old Sloden Wood 25, 27, **118**, 141–6
Old Tame (gardener), conversations with 56–7
Ordnance Survey 32, **73**, **74**, 86, 93, 96, 101

Passford dock 98
Passford Farm 96
Pentridge 40, 89, 125
Picked Post (Picket Post) 52
Pinnick Wood 43, 62, 65
Pitt-Rivers, General Augustus Henry (original name Lane Fox) 64, 76, 78, 79, **117**, 125, 127, 128
Pitts Wood 24, 100, 101, 127, 136, 137, 139, 146
Plumley heathland 50, 52
potters/pottery 34, 67, 100, 101, 125, 127, 136–49
  kilns **18**, 66
  New Forest 100, 101, 104, **118**, 136–49
  potsherds 85
  Roman 101, 136–49
  stamped ware 141
pre-historic men 75
Pre-Raphaelites **10**
Purbeck 40

Quarre Abbey 113

rainfall 20
Rakes Brakes Bottom 62
Redlynch 125
Redshoot Wood 24, 43, 62, 65
religion 87, 91, 107
Ricketts, Charles **10**
Ridley bottom 112
Ridley Wood 25, 27, 102, 109, 110, 112
Ringwood 40, 77, 98
Robin Hood's Clump 53
Rockbourne 19, 20, **117**, 124–9
  origin of name 19
Rockford Common 52, 54, 55, 65, 98
Roden's Bottom 65
Roe Wood Inclosure 64, 65
Roman occupation
  sites 64, 78–9, 125, 129–33, 136–41, 143–9
  villas **117**, 127, 129–33
Romano–British settlements 64, 79, 102, **117**, 124, 125, 127, 128, 130, 132, 137
Romsey 49
Rough Piece, Linwood **118**
Royal Academy of Arts **9**

St Catherine's Hill **9**, **74**
St Ives heathland 50
Salisbury 20, 77
  Museum 123
salmon 35, 38
salterns (salt-pans) 112–14
Saxons 98, 133, 137
  Coronation Benediction 58
  West 79, 85
sea-faring invaders 98
seasons 23
senses, atrophy of 69–70
Setley Plain 107
Shab Hill 34, 38
Shaftesbury 77
Shroton 79
Silchester 117, 130
Sloden 31, 32, 46, 49, 100, 102, 127, 137, 146
  Churchyard **118**
  hill-side Enclosure 100–04
  hill-top Inclosure 101, 110, 145
Slufters 43
smuggling 112
Society of Antiquaries of London **12**, **117**
Solent 112, 114
South Gorley 30, 121
South Tarrant Hinton Down 86
Southampton 130, 136
Spettisbury Ring 86
Spring Pond **17**, 19–22, 124, 125, 127
springs 34 *see also* streams
Standlynch 125
Steepleton 79
Stonehenge 89, 107
Stour, river/valley 20, 80, 119
streams 19–22, 77, 78
Stuckton 52
Stukeley, Dr William (antiquary) 77
Sumner, George Heywood Maunoir (1853–1940) **9–13**
  artist **9–13**
  archaeologist **9–13** (*passim*)
  book illustrator **9**, **10**
  countryman **12**, **17–19**, 20–69 (*passim*)
  cyclist **12**, 57, 76
  furniture decorator **10**
  etcher **9**
  excavator 12, 76–77, 130–32
  family **11**
  folk-song collector **10**, **17**
  lawyer **9**
  marriage **9**
  naturalist **17–19**, 19–69 (*passim*)
  notebooks **10**, **18**
  pantheist **17**
  sgraffito artist **10**
  sketch books **9**
  stained glass artist **10**
  tapestry designer **10**, **11**
  topographer **73–4**, 75–113 (*passim*)
  wall-paper designer **10**, **11**
  water-colour artist **18**

Tarrant Hinton Downs 80
Tarrant Valley 86

Test, river 20, 130
Tichbourne, stream 20
Ticketsbury Hill 24, 136
Tisbury 81
Toyd 20
trees and woods **17**, 24–31, 46, 94, 95, 101, 109, 110, 129, 137, 143, 146
apple 67
Austrian pine 24
beech 25, 27, 40, 104, 109, 110
birch 25, 109
cedar 67
Corsican pine 26
crab-apple 25, 40
Douglas fir 24, 26
elm 27, 67
hazel 25
holly 24, 25, 40, 44–6, 55, 62, 67, 104, 110
juniper 127
larch 24, 26, 40
oak 24, 25, 26, 30, 40, 67, 100, 109, 110
plantations 30
rinded 30
Scots pine 24, 26, 30, 31, 40, 64, 67, 100, 109
spindle 129
Sitka spruce 26
spruce fir
sweet chestnut 24, 25, 40
thorn 25, 40, 129
white-beam 25, 40, 129
wood-burning qualities 67
yew 26, 40, 49–50, 89, 129
trout 38
turf and turfcutters 33, 52

Upton, the Hen-pit at 20

venison 44
Verwood 137
heathland 50

Walbury, the Cock-pit below 20
Wallace, W. G. **74**
West Dean 130
Whatcombe 20
Wherwell 130
Whitefield 119
Whitefield Clump 31, 53
Whitefield Plain 54, 65
White Sheet Hill 81
Whiteshoot Bottom 102
Whiteshoot Hill 101
Whitsbury 77
Whitsbury Castle Ditches 83, 86
Williams-Freeman, Dr J. P. (archaeologist) **12**, **13**, 64, **74**, 96, 100
Winchester 77, 130
Winding Stonehard 56
Winterbourne (tributary of Frome) 20
Winterbourne (tributary of Stour) 20
Woodcuts 78, 79, 125, 128
Woodyates 79, 83, 87, 128